Consecration in the Refiner's Fire:
A Thirty Day Journey

Sean R. Foster

Cover art by Russell V. Slade, Sr.

ISBN: 978-0-578-37445-1

Dedication

To Yeshu'a Ha-Mashiach (Jesus the Messiah) to Whom all glory, honor and power belong. I praise and thank You for trusting me with Your gifts, talents and blessings.

Foreword

When I was given the honor to write the forward for *Consecration in the Refiner's Fire: A Thirty-Day Journey,* and I began to read these prophetic words, the Kingdom of God inside of me leaped and is still leaping!

From Genesis to Revelation, we see the heart of the Father is to restore His people back to worship, an intimate relationship with him. *Consecration in the Refiner's Fire: A Thirty-Day Journey* is about understanding true worship, which is the heart of God. This journey is about tapping into heavenly realms which are already within you. It is not just another thirty-day journey. This book teaches us how to access the realms of God through worship. Many have been asking God how to access His presence in a practical manner. Sit back and buckle your spirit seat belts. You are about to take a ride in the realm of the Supernatural. God is calling His worshipers to tap into the realm of God that is already within you (Luke 17:20-21).

I agree with Sean's definition of consecration. According to Minister Foster, consecration means *"To be devoted to a purpose with dedication or deep solemnity."* I think of consecration is more than pulling away from something. Moreover, it is more about the lost art of relationships that many have pulled away from or placed on a shelf. God is calling His people back to their first love-God Himself. There is coming a great revival and move of God in the body of Christ like never before.

God is not looking for those who desire an easy way out or only sacrifice what is easy for you to do without. He is looking for those willing to consecrate in the refining fire that cost you something. David replied to Araunah, *"for I will not present burnt offerings to the Lord my God that have cost me nothing"* (II Samuel 24:24).

This book was given to this Prophetic Author, Sean R. Foster, an anointed worship leader to worship leaders. It is also meant for everyone who has the heart to build an intimate relationship with the Father. Enjoy the journey and know that God has personally invited you to take a thirty-day journey with Him if you read this book. You have been summoned.

Apostle Brenda H. Ward
Believers Heritage Kingdom Training Center
Cobbs Creek, Virginia

I want everyone reading this to know that I am just a simple man who, amid my deepest flaws and shortcomings, has a burning heart for Jesus Christ. I am not an example for anyone to follow or mold themselves after because I am a human in flesh doing all he can to please a flawless and holy God. Don't see me as a role model or anything else except a servant of the Most High. I make mistakes; I don't always do the right things, nor do I always live my best life. That's the truth. My prayer is that you follow the Jesus I chase after because it is He who will be the template for your life and for this Consecration journey. This book isn't about doctrine or traditions but is based on deepening a relationship with the only true and living God. I am still chasing after God, and I need to continue to do so in each moment of my life. I need His Perfection and I need His Guidance in my existence as I am not any different from anyone else.

In my wildest dreams, I never would have thought that I would attempt to write a book, as I am not that kind of writer. Writing lyrics and poetry are one thing, but a book is a whole different animal, and I am being obedient to what God has been leading me to do. I sincerely pray for your patience and your grace as you read these pages and prayerfully God will use them to bless you. I can truly say that writing this book has opened my eyes to many things I've never had to experience as a Worship Ministry leader and my other paths in the gospel ministry. I am grateful for the growth that God has given me because what doesn't grow, move, or change is dead.

I'm not doing this for fame or fortune, nor am I doing this for any recognition. I am a background seeking person who would rather see the Name of Jesus be more famous than my own. Even if no one would ever remember that I wrote this little book and it got tossed in the corner and forgotten, I pray that someone gleans something from the scribblings of this unworthy vessel. Jesus is the focus and the center of my life and if it weren't for Him, I would be lost and careening towards a real and burning Hell. My life as a worshipper is my passion and as flawed as I am, I realize how much God loves me despite me, so serving others in any way that this imperfect vessel can help I will do what I can. We are all one body in Christ and we all should bear each other's burdens and pick up our brothers and sisters in Christ wherever they are in their journeys (Galatians 6:2).

Regardless of where I have been or what I have done, my goal has been to help anyone I can along the way. Being an aid to others is a ministry all within itself. Being a servant in ministry is important to me because it is when we serve others is when we learn how to lead and teach others what has been given to us. I don't believe that you can be any sort of ministry leader unless you first know how to serve one. You can't be a teacher until you have the discipline to be a student. God put me here to advance His Kingdom, and that is exactly what I am going to always try to do for Him. It refreshes our spirits when we work in and for the Kingdom.

I may not have lived as long as many other great pioneers have lived or done as much as they have done, but God has given us all different viewpoints and voices and He allows us all the space to share with the Body of Christ. I have been playing instruments, singing, directing choirs, leading praise and worship and serving in music ministry for thirty years, starting from my teenage years until the present. God has had to grow, groom and whip my stubborn self into holy submission and through it all, God has blessed me and taught me, and I will always continue to allow God to do so. I am always in His class, and I will always seek His teaching and guidance.

There is much I have learned and yet so much more that I don't yet know or have understood. However, the Greatest Teacher in the Universe continues to place me in situations where He has either clearly spoken or amplified the knowledge He has given me and He alone. I recognize the futility of my existence without Him. I still make mistakes and I still get frustrated and even angry when I make them. I've learned to accept that it's in my weakness that God shows Himself to be strong (II Corinthians 12:9).

In planning for a special worship encounter for the church that I (at the time of this writing) am currently serving as a Minister of Music I believe God encouraged me to these thirty days of devotionals not only to share with my team but to share with anyone else who is looking for a framework or starting point that they can use to begin a journey into the Heart of Christ. This isn't a ceremonial voyage or one that needs to be done publicly so that people can see how holy they are. No one should do this sort of thing to puff their chests out to say how "holy" they are. No, this is about embarking on a trip into and expanding the relationship we have with Jesus. If your goal is to show people just how super-saved and super-righteous you are to others? Put this book down now until you get it right with God. This is about truly growing in relationship with God. Nothing else.

Over the years, I have had my eyes opened to many truths that God has revealed to me about building up His Kingdom on Earth. I feel that many of us have lost our first love. So many people are focused on building "empires" of ministry and have lost their focus on the thing that should bind us to God first, which is a deeper relationship with Jesus Christ. I am reminded that the First Adam walked with God in the evening's cool and the Second Adam walked among us on the Earth. We need to get back to living day-to-day with God and serving Him with all of our heart, soul, and mind. We need to do whatever we must do to get in the places that God has for us to serve in. We cannot do that ordinarily because we in the flesh must be prepared on a spiritual level, which requires us to do a unique thing to get a different result.

I wrote this book for the worship leader, but it can apply to anyone in a ministry capacity with a heart that is open to God. Every person who serves God needs to have consecration periods in their lives. Consecration isn't just for official positions or titles in ministry. Consecration is a covenant between God and us humans to be set apart and prepared for God's use wherever we are. Regardless of what you do in ministry, we should want to be purified and prepared for God to use for whatever He wants us to do for Him and be for Him. Our lives have an ordained purpose and destiny, and God has laid out the plans, but it is up to us to accept the challenges and move forward as He has desired for us (Jeremiah 29:11).

I have learned many hard lessons during my time serving in music ministry, and God has revealed many things to me as I have served. I have been plunged into the Refiner's Fire many times and I've had many pitfalls, bumps and bruises along the way, but the one thing that I have consistently done is draw closer and closer to God. Most of the time I feel like a screw-up, but God has reminded me that He knows, and that He loves me anyway, despite my shortcomings. When I began to truly understand how important what we as the workers in ministry are so important to building the Kingdom of God on Earth versus just packing in a church house is when the big picture was unveiled. We can't take this likely, and our adversary will take advantage of us and mow us down if we don't know how to take our rightful place by God's side.

Being in the right position is everything. I can't say that enough. Being where God wants us to be in Him is the critical component so many miss working in ministry. Just because we have talents doesn't mean that we are in the right place with God. Being able to sing, play instruments, or preach the paint off the walls doesn't matter. Whatever we can do well in human eyes does not mean an automatic alignment with God. It just doesn't work that way. We are the ones out of place. We are the ones separated from God because of sin. We are the ones that have to go back to the Father because He is God. He is the standard. We have to push our flesh aside and realize that it is not nor never will be about us. Some of what we do for ministry will bring us into human circles of popularity and we have to be careful not to let it get to our heads.

We cannot allow ourselves to be blinded by the lights of fame or made complacent with the status quo of ordinary. I can't find a single place in the Bible where we are to remain still or think that we have arrived, except at the end of the Book of Revelation, where the conclusion of time is recorded. I have had discussions with my brothers and sisters in Christ, witnessed the operations of ministries from the inside and out and God dropping nuggets in my spirit about how to navigate this road towards His high calling in Christ Jesus (Philippians 3:14). On top of all of that, God gave me the gift of teaching, which allowed me the ability to show others what God has shown me. Once you allow yourself to see what God has in store, you can't hide it and you can't deny it anymore. You must tell everyone that will listen in season and out of season (II Timothy 4:2).

It is the truth of God that makes us free (John 8:32). There is no way that our version of what we think is the truth will stack up to a hill of beans (as my Dad used to say). In my time on this earth, I have had to look beyond the fluff and dig for the actual reality. Learning to look past titles and latitudes and beyond accolades and affirmations, God has always shown me the way. Many times, I didn't want to listen or acknowledge what He showed me because of traditions or my fear of rocking the boat. Every time I wanted to cower in fear, God would give me the strength to stand up for what was right. Many times, through rebuke, rejection and being undermined, I never lost sight of what God has placed me here to do and I may not have always been understood, but God was filling me up with His Wisdom. I knew I couldn't keep it to myself anymore.

I started jotting things down in apps on my cell phone so that I wouldn't forget them. Anything from "ah ha" moments of personal revelations to conversations that I had with my brothers and sisters in Christ. I did all I could to keep journals and notebooks of whatever it was God showed me or revealed. After compiling these thoughts and principles, I truly believe that I heard the Lord say: *"Put it in a book"* and I followed suit. I started writing and writing and I didn't stop. I honestly couldn't stop. My brain went into overdrive, and I started having dreams about things great and small. I said nothing to no one because I didn't want to ask people for prayers and support for this if I didn't finish it (yes, I know, but I am still human), but I took it one day at a time. I asked God for strength and wisdom.

This book began with a message for my Team for the first day of devotionals in preparing for our event. Our Team uses an instant messenger client to share songs, information, devotionals and teaching. I remember writing that first day in the Teaching section freehand and hitting that send button with all the fear and nervousness you could imagine. I waited and saw no movement and it was the hardest two hours I could imagine. Then there was one like, two likes, and then the comments came in. They told me how blessed they were, and I felt so relieved. I thanked God repeatedly because I knew I couldn't have done it without Him. Then reality reminded me that this was just the first day, and that I had twenty-nine to go. It was at that moment that I knew I needed God's help.

I kept praying and believing that God would provide exactly what I needed. Day after day, I prayed and meditated on God. Before I would even know that this was going to become a book, I would continue to write the devotionals and make notes on the side, and this thing was getting bigger and bigger. I eventually had to graduate from my cell phone, journals and notebooks to the computer as writing and editing became more difficult, staring at a tiny screen and having things in different places. God showed me things to build around the devotionals and before I knew it, multiple chapters had been written and I didn't stop until I felt God say that it was enough.

When the thirty days were over and we held our special worship event, we all led worship like we never had before. The Spirit of the Lord fell on that place and lives were transformed by the power of the Holy Spirit. I saw the glint of excitement in their eyes, and I witnessed the growth in their personal ministries. I knew it was all God's doing, and I also knew that I did what God had told me to do. Even though we were a small team and insignificant in human eyes, God reassured me that releasing these writings for His Glory to help build His Kingdom is what I had to do, and here we are today.

My flesh was (and still is, to a small degree) hesitant. I hope I can be transparent about that, because the one thing we need to remember (repeatedly) is that we are in the flesh. We have to rely on the Spirit of God to do His Will. Being obedient is hard, but when we do what God says? It changes everything and it changes us. Growing more in Christ and consecrating ourselves for His purpose and Glory will do that to us in ways we cannot imagine.

So, I earnestly ask that you pray for me, the author, as my road of relationship with Jesus is always growing and ever-changing as I grow closer to Him. Being in a deeper relationship with Christ is the goal whether you are preparing for a worship event, a worship service, or just in regular life. Let God grow you and take you where He wants you to go. Whether it be through the valley, the desert or the abandoned place, trust God in all things. There is only one way to Jesus, but the road we travel may be longer, have unique experiences, or be out of the ordinary. The path we take and the lives we live are according to His master plan for us. Only God truly knows.

CONTENTS

Acknowledgements

I want to take a few moments and thank God, who is my Lord, Savior, Master, Friend, and the source of my life and strength. Without Him, I am nothing and never would have or would be. To God be all the glory for the many wonderful things He has done. I know I am not famous or standing in the circles of celebrities, but I bless God for His inspiration to collect these thoughts together and put them out to the world as He inspired me to do. If only one person reads this book and only one life is changed, I have done what God has asked me to do. What I do for the Kingdom of God on Earth is so that Jesus will be made famous and not me. God deserves all the glory and not me, because I don't want it. God is so much greater than I ever could be, and I freely give it up to Him because He is worthy of all the praise.

To my beautiful wife, my Queen, my companion and my best friend, the one and only Mrs. T. L. Foster. We first connected over music and ministry, as she is a wonderful soloist who has lived and breathed music all of her life. We grew up together on different paths until high school and years later, here we are married and in love. How you and our daughter would sit behind me in whatever church I am in while I lead praise and worship and shake a fan, wipe my brow or give me water. There is NOTHING like a wife that loves and supports your dreams and walks beside you in ministry (and I mean NOTHING). Thank you, Honey for always being there and encouraging me as we grow together.

As a worship leader and a musician, my words of thanks go to not only spiritual and ministry mentors, but to some secular ones as well. God brought people from many areas into my life to grow me and to challenge me to reach higher and I am grateful to them all because we are all the sum of many parts. There are SO MANY other people I want to thank for sowing into me and giving me the chances to thrive and do what I was created to do. Besides

God above, I want to thank my Dad the late Deacon James Foster, and my Mom Mother Clemmie Foster, who raised us in the ways of The Lord and kept music flowing in our house. To my brother Elder Alexis Foster, my "dynamic duo" musician partner, I am always forever grateful for your love, your musicianship and being your brother. To my sister Shanell Foster, who is a gifted vocalist and musician herself, words cannot express how your wisdom, grace and powerful singing voice and love for ministry flows out of you. I also love being your brother. All of us together were The Foster Family and I will never forget all of our sessions around that old kitchen table (which I still have!) From my Dad playing guitar to Mom singing in her outstanding contralto voice, music is in our blood because of our parents. They were not perfect, but they chased a perfect God and it rubbed off on us. The same goes for my human bloodlines of the Fosters, the Gwynns, the Joneses, the Lees, the Wares, and all of their extended families of the Tidewater Region of Virginia. The amount of music, talent, and ministry that flows from these families is immeasurable. God blessed me to be a product of bloodlines that endured many tribulations and overcame them all with the Lord's help.

To my Apostles Dwayne and Brenda Ward, who have been my encouragement and foundation in the years that I have known them, I am so grateful to you both for your wisdom and leadership. You both do not know how much you have influenced me up close and from afar. You both have lit a fire in me to grow the Kingdom of God as Christ gives me the ability. Thank you for always being there for me and for sharing examples of what ministry needs to be. I am so grateful that God brought you both into my life and into the lives of the Believer's Heritage Kingdom Training Center in Cobbs Creek, Virginia. I can't wait to see y'all on TV one day!

To my home church, the Zion Baptist Church of Cardinal, Virginia, and to her pastor, I am grateful for my start and foundation. Zion Baptist Church has been the epicenter of many great and influential musicians and vocalists that have served there (especially the group 4 One Purpose). I have had so many mentors in my hometown of Mathews, Virginia, and the surrounding areas I will never forget, and I am thankful for their mentorship up close and from afar. From the musicians and singers I watched growing up to the influential teachers and educators that poured music into me, I am so appreciative.

I also would like to thank all of my musical friends who attended the greatest Historically Black College and University on the planet with me, which is the one and only Hampton University (THE REAL HU) and its amazing legacy of musical excellence. I didn't attend Hampton for music, but I knew many of the vocalists and musicians there that affected my life. There is one brother I would like to honor his memory, and that was my friend James A. Sellers. James had a magnificent voice and a big heart. Many nights, all of my musical friends would assemble around James' massive CD collection and sing gospel music (especially Commissioned) into the wee hours of the morning. James also encouraged me to stop hiding behind my shyness and play music and sing without fear. His passing took us all by surprise and hurt those of us that knew him deeply. My only regret is that he said that if I ever recorded a project that he would sing background vocals on it for me. I'm sorry we never got that chance before he transitioned.

To my Maryland crew, the Judah Worship Ministry that I have been honored to lead, I thank you for making me a better leader and a better Psalmist. To the Restoration Free Gospel Church in Lexington Park, Maryland and her leadership, I say thank you for giving me my first shot as Minister of Music all of those years ago. To the many other skilled musicians and vocalists that I have served with, I say thank you for your kindness and fellowship as we stay connected by the God and ministry we love together. I'm honored to know you, have played music and sang with you all. From the stage to the studio, we have been there for each other in song, in prayer, and in many other situations.

Last, but not least, I want to acknowledge a man who was my friend and a fellow musician who transitioned to be with the Lord years ago. That man was Charles William Brooks, Jr. I will never forget his passion for the Lord and his superb musicianship as we played and served together. I will never forget visiting him before he passed with my friend Russell and how we sang and worshipped in that hospital room. Even to the very end, he was a musician, and I will never forget him. Wow… It's just overwhelming to think of it all!

I also want to thank each of you once again for reading the scribblings of a broken vessel. From the bottom of my heart, I am forever grateful!

A RELATIONSHIP WITH JESUS VS. RELIGION

I know someone somewhere out there is asking themselves why I am opening this book with a discussion about a relationship with Jesus. When you look at the beginning of scripture and of time, the first relationship on the Earth was the one between God and Adam. Right there in the Garden of Eden God has made Adam and spoke with him, walked with him and related to his later loneliness. God had given Adam a job, made him a wife, and wanted them both to be happy. God had a perfect relationship with human beings until sin entered the picture. Because of the original sin, the relationship between God and humans had to be reconciled with His master plan. This blueprint went from God speaking and moving on people as He saw fit to the founding of the Abrahamic Dynasty, to God being born into the flesh as Jesus Christ and the prophetic foretelling of an epic showdown where sin is destroyed, and life eternal would begin. It's all a process and we are just here for our part of the ride.

Ever since humanity was banished from Eden, we all have been collectively trying to understand why things like this happen and how do we relate to an all-powerful God. Just like the thinking people we are, we used our little packages of gray matter to construct a way for us to not fail that badly again. In the early days of humanity, we didn't all draw from the same pool of understanding. People knew that some power existed higher than they were, but because of fear or ignorance attempted to rationalize all of this in terms that they could understand. Religion was born, and many were forced into it as a societal norm because controlling other people is what many humans do. Temples, synagogues and churches have risen and fallen during our small sliver of history and yet God has never changed (Malachi 3:6-8). Even though many faiths don't have all the right details, or some other powers rose and claimed to be God, what we have today in our world is a great big mess.

I look at my own life. I went from being in church all of my life being dragged to church as a child to my ever-evolving state of chasing after Jesus as much as I can as He leads me. When I was young, my parents made going to church a requirement to live in our household (as in with the things that were beyond needs like TV, toys and later cars). It wasn't an option to not take part and believe me; we did what they asked us to do (or else). My siblings and I grew up in a church where we served as ushers, choir members, Sunday School teachers, and I also was a "junior deacon" through my teen years before I went to college. Everyone in our family worked in the church and it was the norm for us. Generations of our family lived in or near the church. Yes, we loved God as a family, but because I had a limited understanding back then, it was all about church attendance and church culture for me.

The relationship I had with the church as a youth was familiar, and I was cool with that. It's what I knew and understood, and most people loved their home churches even if they moved away after growing up. Down in the South, the Homecoming annual observances are a big deal. People came back from wherever they went to remind themselves about what "family" was about. Our church was a community and let me be clear… it's supposed to be a community and it's something that we need more of today. Still, I remember how since my Mom was in the choir how they would prepare special songs for that Homecoming morning service. It wasn't until I paid attention to music and choirs did I begin to learn of a more intimate connection to God.

Let me backtrack for a minute. One beginning of my praise and worship journey was being a member of our family singing group. Music lived and breathed in our home as my father played guitar and many nights we would gather around the kitchen table and sing together. I can still see Dad's black and gold Gibson guitar in my mind, the smell of the gently burning tubes in his Fender amplifier and the gentle hum it made until he flipped the polarity switch to the right setting. I would hear my Dad and Mom singing hymns or whatever the latest Gospel songs that were on the radio. Those nights were filled with so many emotions, from upbeat and inspirational to solemn and heartfelt. I can remember when I was a little tot I would peek around the corner and watch and see the tears flowing and the lifted hands and at the time I didn't really know why. Even my extended family is musical and also firmly grounded in serving Christ and in the church. From the cousin who made his own violin to the many vocalists and musicians that pepper my family tree, church music was (and still is) life to us. Many pastors, prophets, elders, ministers, and evangelists have also come out of our family, so having a foundation in Jesus Christ and the desire to serve in ministry is just who we are as a family. Church was what we did. As a growing young man, I saw and thought I understood what was happening. The cold, hard reality was that I didn't.

One of the major hurdles I had to overcome in developing a personal relationship with Jesus is going beyond the fine line of having a relationship with the church versus knowing Christ Himself. The church is wonderful. The church is a culture within itself. When I was a little guy, I thought everyone had one of two first names: Brother or Sister. I grew up with the church fan that had either the Praying Hands, The Last Supper, Mahalia Jackson or the Rev. Dr. Martin Luther King, Jr. on the front and a funeral parlor advertisement on the back. I can remember the preacher and the choir wearing their fine robes, the ushers that wore gloves, the ceremonial Communion Sunday service with the Deacons wearing white gloves and the Deaconesses uncovering the Sacrament Table with the utmost care and fold the tablecloth with precision and light the candles. I can remember reciting the Church Covenant on 1st Sundays, the Responsive Readings every morning service, Vacation Bible School in the summers and so much more.

The church is powerful and moving. The church was (and still should be and I can't say it enough) the foundational pillar of every community. Back in the olden times, everything happened at the church house. There's nothing wrong with that, so please don't misunderstand me. The problem is that if we aren't rooted in Jesus on a deeper personal level, we can become dependent on what happens on Sundays and mid-week events versus being connected more to Christ. Yes, you can regularly attend the church that is firmly based on Jesus and never truly know Jesus. There are, in my honest opinion, many people that are in church because they were scared into being there. Most people remember being terrified about going to Hell and that in order to get to Heaven that you must be saved. This is true, so don't think I am not against any of this. The issue is HOW someone was converted because I think many got "saved" out of an emotional response to fear (or tragedy) and gave their life to the church versus feeling convicted in their spirits and giving their life to Jesus. Remember, I said that there is a fine line, and it is often very hard to see.

I've had to go through a lot of hard times and experiences to truly understand that while fellowship in the church is so needed and beneficial it is those moments with Jesus in the midnight hour or an hour the church house isn't open or the pastor available that deepen that relationship with Him. I love my Pastors and I love my church, and especially when I grew up, I encountered God, and a relationship was born there. I won't forget any of that, nor will I minimize the impact. You can never forget where you started.

Yet, I have encountered so many people who seem to only thrive when the church is open. They seem to languish and suffer so many things when the doors are closed. I'm not slamming anyone here, but I'm just being honest because I was there too at one time. I had a relationship with the church that was stronger than the one I had with Christ. It's easy to do that because I can see the Pastor and I can see the people. I can feel the Spirit when the service is high. My senses can feel God moving and for many, that's all they learn. They don't know that this is only the beginning. This is just the appetizer to a very large and intricate meal.

It wasn't until I went to college that I experienced God away from my home church on a deeper level. Now, before anyone reads this and knows where my home church is, let me be clear about something. I am not bashing or slamming them. Every ministry grows and changes over time, just like anything else. My home church has developed from the traditional and stoic and has crossed over into an even more spiritual house where the five-fold ministry is at work. They changed as a church, just as I did in those campus ministry encounters. Those campus groups did something I didn't understand then like I do now... They loved to worship.

Growing up with choirs and gospel quartets was my musical foundation. I still enjoy them, and they are still powerful forces in the church. I remember people lifting their hands or standing on their feet. Hands clapping and foot stomping music with tambourines going was what I experienced as a wide-eyed child. I remember the heart-wrenching music that moved people to where they would cry, shout, dance and get "happy" and get surrounded by ushers who would fan them or walk them out of the service because it "distracted" those who were enjoying the performance (I use this word on purpose). This is what I knew until I went to these meetings in college.

What I witnessed in those campus ministry meetings at first seemed "scary" to me. People dancing, crying, standing, or on their faces before God was something I wasn't used to seeing. People speaking in tongues and hearing others give words of knowledge and prophetic utterances were unusual to me, but it intrigued me. I witnessed people who were singing songs about Jesus that spoke of how they loved Him so deeply. They sang old hymns in ways I never did before. They ministered familiar songs in styles I had never encountered before. They were beyond emotional, and I wanted to know more. I wanted to experience this to a greater degree, but I knew I couldn't just flip a switch and have that sort of encounter. Honestly, looking back, it started long before college. I just didn't realize it.

When I was fifteen and beginning my journey as a church musician, I was fascinated (I still am) by King David. David was a man after God's Heart. David was a fantastic Minstrel (musician) and Psalmist (lyricist and worshipper). He wrote songs that captivate billions around the world to this day. His life story as a misunderstood child and outcast resonated with me personally. I was an oddball geeky church kid, so just use your imagination. Back then, I didn't know any better, and I earnestly prayed to God to have David's anointing because I knew what anointing was. I knew David had that "thing" that only God could give to him. I asked God for what I didn't fully understand. I had not one clue that I had asked God for not just David's talent, but that I had asked for his tribulations, too. I asked for what David endured as a boy and then what he went through as a man. I can honestly say that when I realized my error, I regretted praying that prayer. However, as I've gotten a little older and wiser, I am thankful to God that He answered my prayer as I grow and learn on this journey that God made just for me.

To make a long story short, that encounter with praise and worship in those campus ministries stuck with me and incubated within my spirit. Years later, after I graduated college, got married, and all that while I was still going to my home church once a month to play one Sunday and lead a choir. It was great, and I enjoyed it. Then one day my now former father-in-law was moved upon by God to start a ministry and he asked me if I would be his Minister of Music and to create a "Praise Team" with a multicultural appeal. I accepted the challenge, and that's what I did, and we began singing songs of various artists and did so with fervor and feeling. Then one day a lady who was visiting the church said she was moved upon her heart to give me a CD to listen to because God had said to give it to me, and she wanted to be obedient. That CD was by Matt Redman and was titled *Facedown* and it changed my life once again.

I devoured that recording, and the feelings I felt back in college resurfaced. It was around that time that I had experienced some dark times in my life and that CD came at such a pivotal moment. My trials had become too much to bear, and I began searching out other artists that spoke of loving Jesus in such a deep and personal way. They were using Psalms and scriptures that I had heard before in ways I never experienced so deeply. They sang words of adoration and testimony that shifted the atmosphere in my life. I listened to my trusty MP3 player (remember those?) filled with this music and it transformed me.

Not only was I listening to this music and teaching it to my team, I started praying more, but I also read the Bible more. Then my life spun out of control, and I dealt with one tragedy after another. My health had taken an ugly turn, my first marriage was crumbling, and I had gotten laid off from my job for nearly nine months. I went from having a decent living to requesting public assistance to eat and heat my home. I went on countless interviews and couldn't find a job no matter what I did. I was slinging food out of a food truck, working twelve and fourteen-hour days just to make a hundred dollars. I had a mortgage that was behind, bills that were overdue, and a home that lost running water because the pump that was down in my well had blown up. My car was broken down and so was my spirit. Life was bleak, but God was still there.

Because I didn't know what else to do, I prayed all the time. I prayed while driving and I prayed when I was home. I prayed whenever I could. I buried myself in God's Word thanks to Bible apps and online content. Life seemed hopeless, and I prayed constantly for my situation to change. I prayed for relief for what pain I felt and even that changed. I worshipped at church and privately at home, and things shifted in me and around me. I stopped praying for what I needed, and I started praying to God about me drawing closer to Him. I started to just pray to glorify Him, and my heart changed. I stopped seeing my situation and saw God everywhere.

I understood how when I was unemployed that people would always come up and give me money or invite me to dinner. Every time it seemed the cupboard was bare, there was always one more meal to be made. I kept seeking God. Then I found myself not praying for myself, but praying for others. I felt differently about everything. When no one else could assure me that things were going to be okay, God would show me He was on the case. I sought a deeper level in Him. I would fall to my face in awe of His Glory and power. I blessed the Name of Jesus and I poured out my heart unto Him because I knew only He could truly understand me. Then one day, God did something unexpected.

Zephaniah 3:17 details that God spoke or sang over His people. I never knew what that meant until it happened to me. I was worshipping God alone, and I had a Jacob wrestling the angel kind of moment. I didn't want to let go of God until He blessed me. Not with material things, but to show me He was truly real. My mind flashed back to those college days. I remember those people seeming crazy, but I knew they had something I wanted. I wanted to see and experience God in that way, but I wanted to see Him for myself. Then it happened. Not in an English language sort of way, but in the deep vibration of my spirit. Glimpses of things to come and God showed Himself to me in ways I never knew before. I felt no shame before God. I felt His love, and I felt His embrace. The creator of the Universe knew my name. He knew my pain, and He knew my faults, and it didn't matter. His love was so real I could taste it. His power was overwhelming and all I could do was fall to my face and weep. There was no music playing, no song being sung, but my spirit took over and cried out loudly to the Most High God.

My flesh lost the battle to hold me back. Aches and pains vanished. The urges of hunger and the call of the restroom ceased to be heard. I just wanted MORE of God. My hunger for His Presence was overwhelming and all-consuming. I didn't even truly know what that meant in those moments, but I knew I was safe, and I knew God was as real as He could get. Time stood still. Hours went by and when I came to my senses, the darkness of the night had set in. It was daylight when I began this experience, and I didn't even know that several hours had passed. It was amazing, and I wanted more.

Even after that encounter, I experienced much pain in my life. I still had struggles. I had even more pain on top of old pain. My first marriage ended badly and was headed to divorce. My heart was split in two. My spirit was crushed, and my hopes were dashed. I stopped leading worship because I felt I was irretrievably broken. I left my position as Minister of Music at the church, quit my appointment as a deacon, and went into a shell. I would come home on a Friday after work and wouldn't leave the house until Monday morning. I would sit in the dark crying until my tear ducts would swell shut. My soul was shredded, my faith shattered, and I didn't want to be alive anymore. I would sit in the dark in my house and would only move to go to the bathroom. I would often think of how many ways I could end my life. I could see the headlines about how I was found after being dead for weeks because I felt no one would care enough to check on me. The devil really had me bound and he was laughing at me. What I didn't know was that God had me in His Refining Fire. He allowed these things to happen, and He allowed the Devil to laugh in my face.

I had given up, but God never gave up on me. God kept knocking at the door of my heart. He wouldn't abandon me even though I gave up on life. My best friend, Russell, would always check on me. Many times I didn't answer the phone. He would leave me voicemails encouraging me. Telling me to fight on like I had told him when he was going through his storm. He would come by my house and just sit with me. He prayed for me (many times at my front door because I wouldn't let him in). He wouldn't let me go, and I know God used him for my healing. He reminded me I had told him how good God was when he was going through. How I had prayed for him when he was down, and I remembered that same God that I encountered for hours alone at my old house. I remembered that same God and my strength returned.

It was because of my relationship with Jesus that I am alive on this Earth. I will never forget how He restored my faith in Him. Got me back into leading worship again. Surrounded me with people I needed for that season as God rebuilt me brick by brick. The fire on my altar had smoldered, but it never went out. I got divorced and I found joy and happiness flourished once again. I eventually got a better job closer to home and gave up commuting for the first time in ten years. I went back to my hometown to visit my parents one Easter weekend and reconnected with a woman that I hadn't seen in twenty-five years, and we fell in love, and we got married. God had remembered my tears and He recalled that my heart still burned for Him, and life turned around. God turned my setback into a comeback! His perfecting work in the Refiner's Fire had done its perfect work!

This snippet of my story is just one example of why a relationship with Jesus versus just the church is so very important. I almost let go. I had given up, but just like any loving relationship where one of us withdraws because they are hurting, the other reaches out and does all they can to make it better. God is no different. When we go beyond the initial connection we experienced when we first got saved and seek God for more than what we need or want and want to get to know Him for ourselves? Things happen. Changes happen. God becomes more real than reality itself.

In any relationship, there are major pillars that make them work. Two of them are communication and intimacy. In our spiritual lives, prayer is communication and worship is intimacy. When we pray, we talk to God, and we converse with Him (because He talks back). Too often, we only pray when we want something, but prayer is much deeper than that. We can pray to talk to God and seek more of Him. We can share with God (even though He already knows) and speak with Him like a child can to their father. We can even just talk to God and not ask anything at all. Prayer is just like a cell phone. We can call on God for whatever we want, need, or just to chat. It's really that simple.

Now, before someone goes off the deep end about how intimacy with God seems a little weird, I get it. Until I understood all of this, it made little sense and seemed a little... Creepy. The first thing most people who don't understand worship hear the word "intimate" and think of the word "sex" and that's just wrong. They hear some worshippers call God "Daddy" and they immediately condemn worship as we know it now as some sort of heresy. Here's what I understand now. The Word of God and worship are how we can be intimate with God. Look at human relationships for a moment. We get closer to people when we learn about them. The Bible shows us who God is and how He has worked with and through people. When one plunges into His Word, we can see His character, His love, and His grace. We can see His devotion to us flawed creatures.

Worship is a spirit-to-Spirit communion that goes beyond human understanding. We are spiritual beings living in a physical world. When God created Adam, He had a direct connection with him that lasted until the first sin. Through prayer, the Word, and worship, we can connect to God directly. Beyond our senses and limitations. In worship, we pour our love out on Jesus and we transcend the natural world and enter the Spirit realm. God is a Spirit, and this is how we can connect with Him, not through a church building address or a pastor, but just you and God, and that my friends is INTIMATE!

With these pillars, a relationship will grow and flourish. When we connect with God on a deeper level, God reveals Himself more and more to us. He wants us to develop a relationship with Him, as He has given us the tools and the means to do it. He desires us with His endless love and our love for Him should burn and never go out. Without a deep relationship with Jesus, life is meaningless. Life is rudderless and pointless. One certainly cannot do ministry effectively without a deeper relationship with Jesus. I cannot say enough how important this is.

A relationship with God isn't just about knowing Him when we are in trouble. Too often, many church folk only seem to connect with God when Hell rises in their lives. When the good times are rolling, they seem to forget

God, but when the storms of life rage, they fall back on their faces before God and wail and cry at the altar. Mind you, God is such a merciful God that He overlooks our limited view and still steps in on time anyway. Even in our ignorance, He gives us every opportunity to get to know Him better.

Look, I'm not saying that anyone who does this isn't saved or is rebelling against God. We've all seen and been this way before. Look at the Old Testament and see the history of Israel. They worshipped and served God in their troubles and as times got better and after God delivered them; they relapsed into idolatrous ways until they got in trouble and ran back to God again in sorrow asking for His help. God still sees them as the Apple of His Eye, and He feels the same way about us. We were grafted into His family and are joint-heirs with Christ. God never will disown His own. That's a blessed relief!

When we look at scripture, we see how God set up a way for humans to have a deeper relationship with Him. How do you say? Think about this. God went from the invisible God who created the Universe that showed Himself as visible in miracles or significant events to being born in poverty to a teenage girl in a stall where animals were fed and deposited their waste. To grow up misunderstood in the ghetto known for having nothing good coming from it (John 1:46). To walk among us in ministry, performing miracles and being God and human at the same time. This same God who is clothed in Eternity wrapped Himself in flesh sacrificed Himself, enduring one of the worst ways to die humans ever conceived for the sins of every person who has and will ever live.

At the moment of that sacrifice on the cross of Calvary, the great curtain that separated the Holy of Holies was torn in two supernaturally (Matthew 27:51). This curtain that symbolically "contained" the Presence of God from everything else was now gone. Jesus dying on the Cross wasn't just about paying the debt of sin for humans, it was also an invitation to a deeper relationship. Until then, people had to go to the Priest and have sins forgiven, dedicate children, or consecrate themselves. Now, the curtain was torn, and the signal given... God is open to all on a one-on-one basis. God sent the Holy Spirit to teach us all things and bring them to our memory (John 14:26). It changed the game. It gave us access to God in ways that we never could before.

Sadly, humans have a way of messing things up. Our Adversary has a masterful way of manipulating what God breathes into us into a mutated mess. Once organized churches got further and further from those who walked with Christ, more and more humans were convinced that the church had to have power. Some of these power-hungry despots knew if people didn't know that they had a direct path to God that they (religious rulers) wouldn't be needed. With knowledge, there is power. So what did they do? Kept the people blinded. Reinserted the priest in the way of God and made sure that the people wouldn't or couldn't study the Word of God for themselves. Voices who said otherwise were declared as heretics and persecuted. The competition was annihilated and once again, humans were directed away from a direct relationship with God.

If it wasn't for the Reformation, all people under the Banner of Christ would still hold those ideals. God always makes a way for us to get back with Him. Using the Word as a guide, Martin Luther recognized that the way to God was personal. We didn't need the priest and God was closer than we thought He was. Still, God never closed the door on us. He waited patiently and related to us at the level we could understand. God never forces Himself on us, but what He does is leave the door open. He lets us make mistakes as we try on our own to connect with Him, but if our hearts are truly seeking Him, we will find Him (Matthew 7:7-8).

So God has always made a way for us to get closer to Him, even when we didn't know that there was one. He has waited patiently for us and has over all of time been in love with whom He created. If we look at the record, there were and are people that went beyond the normal to have a relationship with God. Some were famous and others were not. Some were in ministry and others were not. We've all seen family members, friends, or even strangers that have had a deeper connection to God. We've seen the evidence of those relationships in things we sometimes didn't understand. Everything from modern-day miracles, blessings upon blessings, and things such as prayer closets, powerful songs, and even art.

The crazy thing is that a deeper relationship with God has always been obtainable. Jesus has been The Way, The Truth, and The Life from the beginning (John 14:6-7). Sadly, we think that a deeper connection with God is a new thing and it's not. God said that He never changes and that means that how we relate to Him doesn't either. However, scripture tells us that in the Last Days God will pour out His Spirit on all flesh (Joel 2:28). As time winds down to an end, the alarm is being sounded that we as people need to get saved and we need to be serious about reaching out to others to be saved before it is too late (II Corinthians 6:2). What I believe is happening is that people outside of the "mainstream" Body of Christ are witnessing the power of a strong relationship with Jesus.

Let's be honest. The Devil is in a fight that he knows he has already lost. Lucifer is a created being just like we are (Ezekiel 28:15). Lucifer had a relationship with God that was deep and meaningful. He stood over the Glory of God and had so much power that pride developed in him (Ezekiel 28:17). He was the closest to God before he fell from grace. The Devil knows how to blend in lies with truth and trick us into using spiritual avenues to connect more to humans and things instead of a forever waiting God who deeply loves us. Why? Simple.

Any person who is deeply connected to God and has a strong relationship with Him is a threat to the Enemy. When we are a genuine friend of God and know that He is our loving Father, there isn't much that can take us away from that (Romans 8:38-39). When we have a deeper relationship with God, our vision becomes clearer. God gives us insights and the Holy Spirit can guide us and reveal deceptions and help us keep our feet on the paths He has for us. We can also see those who are wayward and can embrace our brothers and sisters in love and show them that The Way is clear. God allows us to be the human bridges to an eternal God for others to see.

When we have a relationship with a living God, we can't help ourselves and we cannot contain it. The Prophet Jeremiah said it was like a fire inside of his bones (Jeremiah 20:9). It's contagious and it's beautiful. I would dare say that it's not the church house, a tract, or directed proselytizing (witnessing) that gets the most people to accept Jesus Christ as their Lord and Savior. I believe it is the walking epistles that are you and me living our day-to-day lives in front of other people. It's a sad reality that we may be the only Bible that most people will ever see. Even if people know you deeply or not, they will know that there is something different about you if you have Jesus on the inside of your heart. The closer we are to God and are truly Christ-like (and not pseudo-spiritual and creepy) we reveal to them we are very real, flawed, fun-loving people and that will cause those who don't know Him to possibly see something in us that would make them to ask us what drives us. Who is this God that you know that differs from the other gods and faiths out there?

In our world today there are many other faiths, denominations and paths out there who claim to be the right way into Heaven. I will not debate them here, nor will I "attack" any form of religion, but I will stand on the word of God. Jesus said that He was the way, the truth and the life and that no one came to the Father (God) except through Him (John 14:6). Since Jesus is the gateway we should try to walk like Jesus, talk like Jesus and be like Jesus (I Peter 15-16). We should operate like He did in ministry, and we should relate to others like He did when it came to everything. All of these constructs people have put in place that are intermediaries to Christ need to be removed. Anything that blurs the line between Jesus and salvation is a lie. Anything that adds layers onto what He said Himself is a trap. Whatever tells you that Jesus isn't the authority on Who God is and how God wants us to be is untrue. Run away from that mess and embrace Jesus directly for yourself.

Therefore, a relationship with Jesus is so important. It's not just about us and God (because that is critically important), but it's also about others that can see His good works in us. A genuine relationship with God spills over to everyone around us. Either they will inquire for more or the forces that control them will keep them away. Either way, we have to be the best advertisements for our God. That means the good and the bad. The triumphs and the failures. The accomplishments and mistakes. All while we still chase after Jesus. It makes little sense and it's not supposed to. They see us through pain and glory and still love Jesus. They wonder how this can be possible and people will wonder if we are crazy. We have to demonstrate that not only are we within our right minds, but they too can truly experience all that Christ has to offer them.

Reality is what we can experience and relate to our senses. It's about perception and for us humans, God shows us what is beyond our senses. Others who don't know Him can see God in our lives, whatever they may be. It's a part of God's master plan. It's something that has hidden in plain sight for decades. When we are awakened to what God truly has for us, it is amazing. We are all connected as humans and with God, everything is possible. A relationship with God is also a corporate experience. I mean... Paul wrote letters to churches that were entire cities. Romans, Corinthians, Philippians, and others. They had a relationship with Jesus and together as one. Even scripture says that all of us are the Bride of Christ. Together. All of us. Small and great. Good and bad.

Those of us who serve in ministry need to not just know these things, but live them. Our personal ministries depend on us being authentic and genuine when we go forth and do what we do for The Kingdom. Our world is looking for answers and we, as Christians in Ministry, should be willing to allow God to use us to show others that Christ is that answer that they are looking for. We can't show others what we don't believe ourselves. Even though we have our own soul's salvation to be concerned about we need to have compassion and drive to reach the lost with the good news of God. Ultimately, that's why our relationship with Jesus is important.

For that one who may be reading this right now and they aren't sure that you TRULY know Jesus for yourself or aren't really sure that you are saved I want to offer you some hope. It is never too late to receive Jesus into your heart as your Lord and Savior. There are so many who got "saved" in church because they were scared to the altar, or they were expected at the age of twelve to get saved and they never had a Jesus encounter for themselves. They gave a preacher their hand, but their heart was still lost. I want you to know that it is okay. I have met some who have been going to church for decades and truly didn't know Jesus and today can be your day. You can accept Jesus right now. He is real and it doesn't matter who you are or what you may have done. It doesn't matter what he said, or she said about you. It doesn't matter if you are a sinner or a pastor, Jesus will save you now.

Cry out to God and let Him know that you are truly sorry for all that you have done and that you repent from your sins and will turn from your wicked ways. Earnestly ask Jesus to come into your heart and take His place as the head of your life. Tell God all about your struggles and bare your soul to Him. Tell Him that He is God, and you know that He rose from the dead just for you and just like that you are saved and on your way to Glory!

THE HEART OF A WORSHIPPER

I will not lie. I'm not the greatest authority on this, but God has shown me many things concerning what a worship leader should be. Now as I write this, I know I don't have an international platinum album, nor am I some pastor or great prophet of God that is world famous. I'm just a man with a passion for God and a mission for Kingdom Business. A simple guy that has a heart for God that's always chasing Him despite my many faults and errors. I haven't always been perfect (and I'm not flawless, nor will I ever be faultless), but I've tried to be very transparent. Yet in all of this, I have a massive desire to lead others where God has taken me and hope that God will take them to even higher heights and deeper depths in Him. In the Presence of God is where I have found the greatest peace and the most amazing awareness of who God is. My life's goal is to be of some help to those who want or need the same thing.

I believe that every worship leader should passionately want to lead others into the Presence of God. It's more than just singing some songs before a preacher preaches. However, to lead someone into that blessed Realm of the Spirit of God, one has to already know the way to get there. They have to have experienced the Weight of His Glory bringing them to their knees. Every worship leader should experience the Cloud of His Presence falling in a room. Experiencing the Zephaniah 3:17 moments of God speaking over His people is not an optional thing. Worship leaders should have a fire inside of them they cannot hide. It's not about being selfish and hiding that candle under your bed (Luke 8:16). Worship leaders should have a burning desire to evangelize with the gift of worship to the world.

The sad part about being a worship leader is that, without a doubt, they all go through horrible persecutions and have had terrible experiences in their lives. Trials and tribulations aren't close to describing the depth of hurt, loss, and destruction in their lives. Look up the testimonies of most worship leaders today and you will discover painful pasts (and sometimes presents) of drug use, prostitution, rape, mental torments, broken homes, horrible relationships, torn apart lives, and some things that can ever be repeated or relived. I hear or read their stories and I am amazed that they are even sane or even functioning as people. Yet, they desire to lead others into God's Presence. Flaws and all. They never stop and they won't stop while they are still breathing.

In the lives of worshippers, those dark days lead to a deeper relationship with Jesus. What they learned was that no matter what happens to us, God is still on the throne. Remember the stories of the early Christians being fed to lions? How they were tortured, beaten and sometimes banished for their faith in Jesus? Why weren't they afraid? Simple. They knew that to be absent from the body is to be in the Presence of God (II Corinthians 5:8). Over and over they walked with God, and He never let them down. He never let them go and even in death, they knew that they still had the victory.

A worshipper that is always chasing after Jesus is dangerous to the kingdom of Hell. Therefore, we worshippers are mercilessly attacked, face uncertainties on astronomical levels, and their hearts are broken again and again. Our lives are tormented and never seem to have a single shred of peace. One thing after another comes to make our existence awful and trust me, if you are reading this and think that you're alone, you are not. Believe me when I tell you that many have felt and experienced the same things you are right now. Hell has us targeted for neutralization and destruction. The Enemy hates any of us willing to hold up the Banner of Jesus among the wayward and lost. (I will talk more about this in the next chapter too.) Contrary to what many believe, a worship leader is a minister, just like the ones in the pulpit. We have a mission, and we have a purpose. Many misunderstand it, but believe me, Satan does not. He knows what a worshipper is because I believe he used to be one.

Many Bible scholars believe that the scripture paints us a picture of Lucifer as being a walking instrument (Ezekiel 28:13). If I could use my spiritual imagination, I could see Lucifer as the great worship leader of Heaven. Making music as he walked and he could probably sing the best, write songs that could move the hearts of many. God exalted Him and he stood over the Throne of God and was called the Anointed Cherub that Covered. Yet, he got full of himself and, as the story goes, iniquity was found in him (Ezekiel 28:15). It got to his head, and he boasted from within himself and thought that he should be The Most High and that he was the best of the best. Sound familiar?

Because of this, I believe Satan is good at destroying or misleading worship leaders. I truly believe that he, as the first worship leader, is jealous of us and since he was fired by God, he has a bit of bitterness against his former employer because we took his old job. The best way to undermine a follower of Jesus Christ is to weaken their relationship with Him. Some scriptures detail that some will get into Heaven because God keeps His promises, but some will lose their rewards. They are saved, but because they were led astray, they lose out on some things (I Corinthians 3:14-15). How does this happen? Attack their relationship with Christ. Make all ministers of Jesus weakened, frustrated, and delirious. I truly believe that the Adversary seeks to break the hearts of worshippers and here is why. If the heart is compromised, how can they share any sort of love with anyone? How can I show someone that I love Jesus if I have lost the ability to love effectively? If a worshipper (or anyone in ministry) has not just an emotionally broken heart, but a SPIRITUALLY broken heart, they cannot be effective for the advancement of the Kingdom of God until they allow God to mend their broken pieces (Jeremiah 17:14).

I remember growing up hearing the expression *"new level, new devil"* and I didn't know what it meant until I lived a little while and experienced it for myself. Leaving the world of sin is like a spacecraft launching into orbit. Gravity keeps everything on the Earth. This invisible force will keep pulling at us until we get far enough from it. I've watched many launches and I've seen how much it takes to get something into space. Powerful rockets and engines with tons of fuel and thrust. Those who travel upwards feel the result of the massive push away from the Earth. They experience crushing forces, and they train for months to withstand them. They are taught by those who went before them to teach them what to expect.

I've also seen what happens when those protections and methods fail. I remember as a boy seeing the remnants of planes that crashed because of an accident. Satellites that fell back to Earth because their rockets or systems failed. The fall and crash made things worse than before they lifted off. The force of crashing down to Earth destroys, maims, and even kills. Lives are always shattered forever. Our walk with Christ (just like any other) is one where we lift off from the world of sin and are heading towards Heaven. We don't escape this world until death, and we finally see Jesus. The scripture says that we live in this world but not of it (John 17:11, 14–15). Entering the Presence of God is like flying high in the sky.

Every time we launch our flight upwards to the Glory Realm, this world has the gravity of sin pulling at us. Trying to bring us to the ground again where we started. Worship leaders are no different. We have reached places many haven't, and we want to bring others where we have been. Imagine that we are like the space shuttle. So many precautions were made for each flight. The vehicle was inspected as carefully as humanly possible. I remember when the Space Shuttle Columbia took off for her last flight. It seemed normal and their mission was carried out and when they tried to land, there was an accident and they burned up in the upper atmosphere and all lives were lost. It turned out that a small chunk of foam hit their wing when they launched and punched a hole in their wing's edge[1]. That hole caused high velocity gases to leak in upon re-entry into the atmosphere and the heat and friction melted supports, caused systems to fail and tore the ship apart and they spun out of control as gravity brought them to their graves.

The tragedy was so great that eventually the Space Shuttle program was canceled. Many were demoralized and dejected that the United States Space Program had such a failure. Our enemies LOVED that we had failed and lost dominance in space flight. To this very day, America is still fighting its way back. They realized in the end that the way they had gotten to space was too risky and that new ways had to be found to get there. I know that this is a loose example, but let me try to make this plain. One minor flaw caused the shuttle to fail. The ambition to get to space was just but a little failure caused a mortal ending. It was during the launch that gravity caused a small thing to kill a bigger one and it broke the heart of a nation as people died and jobs were lost. Think about that for a moment. One bad O-ring[2] and one piece of foam on TWO flights out of dozens killed off everything.

When we allow the small things to infiltrate our lives, it can cause us to crash and burn. What may start out as innocent or minute these things can cause us to fail miserably. Now I can imagine that just like anything humans created that there were MANY close calls the Space Shuttle encountered during a flight that the public will never know. Close calls and events were kept hidden from the public to protect the NASA space program. I'm sure that the Apollo Missions had the same close calls that many will never know (and some we do like Apollo 13). I'm sure that many tests and operations have stories out there that could curl or straighten your hair, depending on your situation. In humankind's race for space, so many things could have stopped humans from trying and many actually did, but they carried on anyway.

The same goes for our spiritual lives. Think about it and let's be real with ourselves. How many times have we have "gotten away" with our hidden sins? That bad habit or that illicit relationship. That secret activity or that moral failing. How many times should we have gotten caught? How many times should we have died? How many times did we serve God one hour and willfully sinned the next hour? We still can enter into God's Presence and even lead others there, but in our lives, some things will eventually catch up to us. The Shuttle Program was great and was a feat of engineering and perseverance, but it had flaws that weren't seen until it was too late. It got lax

---

[1] United States., & Godwin, R. (2003). *Columbia Accident Investigation Board: Report*. Burlington, Ontario: Apogee Books.

[2] United States. (1986). *Report to the President. Washington, D.C: Presidential Commission on the Space Shuttle Challenger Accident*.

in its last days and things got passed over and forgotten. Doesn't that seem familiar?

Automobiles are marvelous inventions, and they replaced the venerable horse and buggy, but even cars have been upgraded, changed, and revolutionized. A Model A or Model T might still travel the highway, but a modern car is safer, more efficient, and faster than the pioneering ones of old. Now before anyone says that I'm saying our elders and some traditional ways aren't relevant, please know that I'm not. Here, I'm talking about spiritual relationships with Jesus and not actual people's ages. A relationship needs to develop and grow beyond its beginnings to finish strong.

Every relationship starts as an acquaintance until it reaches the most intimate depths and heights. If we don't work on our relationships, they become stale or worse; they are compromised, and they will fail. The neglect of what was new dies away and we either never let it grow deeper or it falters and fails. New things are developed together to make things smoother and more familiar. In Christ, we have a means to grow in Him as we grow to love Him more. Sadly, our adversary, the devil, knows this too and this is what he wants to prevent.

Our heart is the critical component of this relationship, and therefore it's attacked so much. Therefore, our lives are under the gun at every turn. If we live a sinful life and stay on the ground, nothing will try to pull us back. The higher we go, the more dangerous the fall. There is a major difference between jumping off of one-step versus an entire flight of stairs. When we are called into a ministry role, a fall here is more devastating. How do we know? Because Lucifer FELL from Heaven after God kicked him out. When Adam and Eve sinned, it was called the Great Fall. Falls are devastating. Falls are humiliating. Falls bring pain and injury. Falls also leave bruises and scars.

Let's go back to the worship leader for a moment. We lead others into God's Presence as our ministry. We many times, worship right alongside those we minister to. We know how it feels in His Presence. Because of that, we must stay on guard of our hearts. We must protect our core spiritual beings because if we don't, we could fall. Mind you, fall doesn't always mean that sin is involved. Falling could be that life gets so bad we quit. When a body is injured enough, we lose consciousness and fall to the ground. Falling can occur because of spiritual mistakes or illness.

Those worship leaders with true callings on their lives are targets of the Enemy. He won't rest until he defeats them. He doesn't care that you know Jesus and he will try to trip you up. He is hoping that you don't know what a powerful connection to God is. He hopes you will never reach higher heights and depths in Jesus that will equip you to fight off Hell's traps. He will send stronger and stronger tests to combat you until he succeeds. He has to slow you down and stop you because Lucifer knows he won't beat God, but he wants to rub it in God's Face that he can take down as many people as he can (Revelation 12:10).

Here is a sad fact that might blow your mind. Sometimes Satan uses the church house as his perfect weapon. Yes, you read the right, the enemy will use the place that is supposed to be safe to bring you the gravest harm. I have served in ministries that didn't understand worship or literally persecuted it. True worshippers are labeled as "weirdos" or when worship begins to flow someone, or some situation cuts it off right in the church. I have experienced pastors, bishops and apostles that have zero discernment to the moving of the Spirit unless it is in the way THEY want it to move. Their spiritual eyes are blinded to the workings of the Spirit in worship and treat worship like it's a waste of time.

These ministry leaders and churches seem to do all they can (some unknowingly) to discourage worship and sometimes make worshippers feel like they have done wrong. They drop little hints about the worship team singing "too many slow songs" and use the spiritual dog whistle that they should do more "upbeat" music. These ministries would rather have blaring rock concert or "shouting music" whipping people up into a frenzy so that the congregation is "hyped up" for preachers to preach. I have had some pastors even request that of me for then they speak because they want to come up to the microphone with the praise being high. Instead of wanting what God wants and instead of having spiritual discernment of the Spirit moving they want what their flesh wants, and it hurts that ministry. Out of obedience to authority I have complied, but not without respectfully informing them of their incorrect stance.

I have known people to leave not just worship teams, but whole churches because they are made to feel misunderstood or that they should go elsewhere. These worshippers will be operating correctly in their gifts and callings and God will whisper to them about what He wants to do in the Spirit and their own ministry shuts them down and shuts them out. Their hearts are broken, and their souls crushed because they were only trying to do what God has called them to do. Often it is then that they get dejected and may leave the assignment God has for them too early. If they don't leave a war begins between the worship ministry and church leadership. When that happens the enemy swoops in for the kill and takes advantage of a ministries' spiritual errors. Lives are sadly changed for the worse as that house can go spiritually cold.

Therefore, the Heart of a Worshipper is so important and that it must be protected at all costs. Some days we fail and that's because we are human. Sometimes things fail us, and we need to learn how to survive through God's help. This life is not one of roses and lollipops with sparkling rainbows. It is a hard life and for many; they don't survive. I don't mean physical death necessarily, but their spiritual lights get snuffed down to glowing embers and the Adversary enjoys every moment. The more he can put out the fires in our hearts, the fewer people that can be reached. The fewer atmospheres can be cleaned to remove his hold on those we minister to so that they would freely come and seek deliverance.

The devil won't show up in a sharp red suit with horns and a pitchfork in a cloud of smoke shooting fiery darts at you. No, he will come in your Inbox asking "WYD" or he will come in that sign posted at the liquor store that has a sale on that beer you like. He will come with that blunt that you used to get high on way back when. He will show up in your mirror and tell you that people love your voice or your skill and that you can make a fortune off of them outside of ministry. He will come with that medical diagnosis that it's cancer and you're going to die. He will come when they downsize at your job and somehow you get selected to be fired. He will come when your spouse pulls away from you and runs into the arms of another. He will come when your timing belt breaks and kills the engine in your car. He will come and pick at your smallest weakness and make it bigger. He won't stop and he doesn't fight fair. He will attack you, your spouse, your children, and anyone or anything else he can. He plays the dirtiest pool you could imagine.

He will try to get you to sin or to fall away. He wants to corrupt your heart and remove your zeal. He doesn't have to kill you, but take you down (usually in front of everyone) so that people will see that the God you love so much has "let you down" and if anyone else tried this? They will suffer the same or worse fates. Its manipulation at its finest and Satan is the best at it. The accuser of humanity (Revelation 12:10). The cheat and liar that has weaved his filthy hands into churches everywhere. Disrupting and destroying ministries like it was child's play. He may be strong, but our God is STRONGER.

God has given us a spirit of power, love and a sound mind (II Timothy 1:7). Christ died on the Cross to give us power through Jesus Christ to resist the tricks of the devil (James 4:7). God has given us the tools and we learn those tools through situations the devil meant to break or harm us. We learn to rely on God instead of falling away from Him. The more we rely on Him, the more we know Him. The more we know Him, the closer we get to Him. The closer we get to Him; we learn to protect our hearts. The hearts of worshippers are fragile and on the verge of collapse. We've experienced loss and hurt on levels most haven't experienced, but because we've seen Jesus come again and again not only to rescue us but comfort us and heal us, we learn to never give up on God. Why? Because He won't give up on us!

I'm sure that when you started reading this chapter, you might have been expecting a deep philosophical description of how beautiful this unique thing called our heart is. Well, it's true. It is beautiful and it is marvelous, but it is constantly under attack, and it is so scarred it is a wonder that we can still love God, let alone function. Our fragile heart is being held together by a deep love of Jesus and the light that Jesus puts there makes it into a lantern that seems impossible to exist. A broken heart with more scars that can be counted. A heart that has been trampled, bewildered, and incinerated by life experiences. Yet, it burns for Jesus and shines His Light on everyone they meet. It is a contradiction that makes no sense. That's a worshipper's heart and God and the Adversary both know it.

Here is the odd thing. God never forces us to do anything. God will protect us only if we ask Him to do so. He gives us the Holy Spirit to guide us, and His voice speaks loudly and if we choose to ignore that voice, it will fade into the background. We are beings of choice in the image and likeness of God. If we continually choose God's protection, He will keep us in perfect peace (Isaiah 26:3). It doesn't mean that the weapons of our Enemy won't attack or even hurt us. They just can't win (Isaiah 54:17). The promise God made to us through Salvation can never be broken, but God will allow us to crash and burn if we allow it to happen. I'm sure someone is saying to themselves that God wouldn't let that happen, but God didn't. We did. We allowed it. Every flood starts with one raindrop. Every blizzard with one snowflake. Every forest fire has a single spark. Every fall from grace starts with one poor decision. Every broken heart with a single word or deed.

So we must continually be on guard to our flesh and must ask God to keep us from falling or failing. We must pray for His protection of our emotional and spiritual hearts. God won't help us unless we ask Him to give us what we need to succeed. We will never be flawless like God is, but we need to always be in pursuit of His Perfection and His Desire for our lives. We have to work out our own soul's salvation (Philippians 2:12) and to do that, we have to cultivate Christ into every aspect of our lives and our ministries. It is up to us to reach up to God and to live the way he has prescribed for us to exist for His Glory.

If the Enemy can coerce the Heart of a Worshipper to fail and fall, he wins. We are in the flesh and because of that, we are susceptible to its failings and weaknesses. God always gives us a way to escape danger if we choose to accept it. God also gives us the choice of deepening a relationship with Him that would help us shield our hearts from the tactics of the Enemy. The Heart of a Worshipper is vulnerable because it has suffered for a very long time. It has been often persecuted and misunderstood. It is this vulnerability that allows God to perfect His strength in our weaknesses (II Corinthians 12:9). Beautiful isn't it?

CONSECRATION & CONSEQUENCES

The act of Consecration has many meanings popularized by many churches. When I think about the word consecration I think of it this way:

"To devote to a purpose with or as if with deep solemnity or dedication[3]"

This devotion to the purpose of being a worship leader voluntarily is a declaration to God that you have not only answered His call into this branch of the ministry but that you want to go deeper than the surface level and want to cement your relationship with Him as you deny yourself to prepare to act. As it is a spiritual declaration in a physical realm, it also comes to the attention of the Adversary and with that comes the consequences. You may sweat a little and swallow hard when you see that word "consequences". No one loves consequences. The sad thing is that most of today's churches don't talk about the aftermath of devoting oneself to serving in ministry. Everyone wants the titles and the recognition, but few recognize what one must go through to get to the places that we see the famous worship leaders get to in our world. We see the glory but never know the story.

Personal consecration is a journey of sacrifice and holy commitment. Instead of an object that is being set apart for service, we are voluntarily giving the one thing that we actually don't own, which is our life. We literally have to give ourselves away earnestly as we ask God to take control to mold and shape us into what He desires for us. We have to give up control of everything and let God flip your world upside down. This is not just

---

[3] Consecrate. 2021. In *Merriam-Webster.com*. Retrieved November 8, 2021, from https://www.merriam-webster.com/dictionary/consecrate

submission, but subjection to the Will of God. This is as far beyond ceremonial as the East is from the West. Because we are entering a covenant with God, there are consequences we must face as the direct result of what we committed against God with our eyes wide open. Yes, God forgives, but we must be prepared for the ramifications of whatever we release to God from our old sinful natures. Make no mistake, I'm not talking just about sinners here, but the saved too. We may be redeemed and sanctified, but as we go deeper, we continue to crucify the old self every day (Galatians 5:22-25). As we deepen our walks with God, we deepen every aspect of how we relate to God and how we abandon our flesh.

In the previous chapters, I spoke of the relationship with God and protecting the Heart of a Worshipper and the act of consecration is about submitting to God and deepening our relationship with Him, and to do that we must open up our fragile hearts to God and let Him work on them. Let me be honest with you... This isn't easy, but in a way it is easy. I know that makes little sense, but let me try to explain. When a relationship between two people develops, one of the "side effects" is discovering more about who you are as you discover who the other person truly is. Interactions with them as you increase levels of togetherness reveal the depth of love, the transparency of character, and the unmasking of flaws. I know that this is a very simplistic view, but it is helpful in understanding how a tiny human can enter a relationship with an eternal God.

On a spiritual journey with Christ, we have an uphill climb. It's okay because God already knows this. He's already laid out the way for us because He wants our communion. He made us for just that purpose (Isaiah 43:7). That's why when Adam sinned, God didn't just wipe us out as a failed creation. God came down as flesh to pay for our sins so that we can be reconciled back to Him. The Enemy ruined the first relationship, and he will do EVERYTHING he can to discourage one with God now.

Through every level of consecration and elevation also comes additional levels of anointing. The oil that flows in our lives doesn't just magically appear. How does the oil come from the olive? It comes from being pressed. How does the aroma come out of the rose? It comes from being extracted. How does the steak become nice and easy to eat? It comes from being tenderized or beaten. How do the cells in our body take in nutrients? We have to chew the food, digest it and pass it through our blood. What do all of these scenarios have in common? Transformation.

Imagine that you were shopping for a home, and you see the one you like from the sketch in the builder's display. You choose every option, color and style you want, and you get a mortgage to buy your dream home and when the builder says that it's done, you arrive at your new address and get a massive surprise. Instead of the lovely home you saw in the picture, you see an unimproved lot with a cluster of various types of trees growing, piles of marble and stone, barrels of crude oil and ingots of copper, aluminum and iron instead. The builder happily tells you that this is what you asked for, gives you some blueprints and wishes you the best of luck. I'm sure if this happened in real life you would be ready to sue the pants off of somebody.

In order for a home to be built, things have to be transformed. Living trees die to become cut lumber. Crude oil gets refined into plastics and extracts. Ingots of iron and aluminum get transformed into various alloys. Copper gets turned into wires and other elements into other components. Things are combined and assembled with strict specifications. All of this happens before a builder can assemble them. Everything in a home comes from something on the Earth. Its refinement was grueling and took it from its original form into what was desired by the builder. With a home renovation, the builder removes what is rotten, dilapidated, and unwanted and replaces it with the new components according to the blueprints.

God takes us as raw materials and makes us over again; except we have a say in whether it happens. The trees can't tell the lumberjack no thanks. I will just stay here and grow. The iron cannot protest being heated, mixed and melted. Raw materials in the natural realm have no voice or opinion, but we as humans do have such an opinion and voice because God won't transform you unless you allow Him to do so. God is not a rapist (yes, I said it). He will not force Himself on you and won't change you unless you ask Him to. The reason being is that we have a personal relationship with Him. He is still God Almighty, but He has given us the ability to choose to go forward or backward in His plans for us. The act of Consecration cannot happen without SUBMISSION!

Remember that part where we spoke about relationships growing and that part about the revelation of oneself as two get closer? Well, this is where it gets interesting. God has no character flaws, nor does He have any negative traits. All of those things come from us humans who were born in sin and shaped in iniquity (Psalms 51:1-5). The Enemy doesn't want to see us get closer to the God that threw him out of Heaven. Satan is a bitter, jealous and jilted being. He rebelled against God and truly hates us for those of us who dare to be a worship leader or ministry servant. He sees our journey and has a plan to stop it. Those are the consequences.

Scripture says that Satan is the accuser of humanity (Revelation 12:10). Remember, part of a deepening relationship is learning who you truly are. The Enemy always steps right in and forcefully reminds us of our flaws. He assaults our characters. He rains down showers of guilt and low self-esteem on us like you wouldn't believe. His goal is to make us feel unworthy of God's Love. To feel like God could never use us because of what we've done in our pasts or even our present. Every trick he can try, he will use. From shaming us to tempting us with our weak points. He becomes every roadblock and hindrance he can be and trust me... He doesn't fight us fairly.

When we submit ourselves to be consecrated, we enter a spiritual battlefield and, for first-timers, this can be a worst-case scenario. Spiritual warfare is intense, grueling and real. We aren't fighting humans here (Ephesians 6:12). Humans are involved, but this war is fought in a realm we have been made unaware of because of our flesh. Our five senses aren't equipped for the spirit realm, but thanks be to God that the Holy Spirit gives us a glimpse of that world. He gives us the time-tested toolset to win. To use those tools requires us to tame our flesh and our humanity as we allow ourselves to be integrated into God's Spirit.

So, yes, we are at war, and we are outmatched and outgunned as humans. Hopefully, you don't get discouraged when you read this. Let me be real with you... I was terrified at first and I won't lie; it was tough, and it was a serious reality check. It still is and I believe that it always will be. The Enemy will attack your mind with crazy and damning thoughts. He will attack your body with sickness and pain. He will stir up passionate desires to sin. He will tickle your addictions with temptations. He will attack your family and cause Hell to rise in your home. He will attack your finances. It could get deep and nasty. It could get Job-level crazy and sometimes much worse.

Just like we talked about gravity, the more we pull away from our pre-ministry lives, the more the Adversary will fight us at every turn. The higher we go, the stronger the fight. In every way, God leads us to evade defeat that old devil will try another means to stop you. It never ends. It won't stop until we die and transition to Heaven. Sorry to disappoint you. It's just the truth that most people don't want to hear. People see worship leaders and love their anointing. They see the Power of God flowing through every note and every movement, but they do not know how much that oil cost them. They do not know how many sleepless nights they endured. How many times their heart was shattered into dust. They couldn't calculate the amount of loss they had had to experience. There are so many that have survived things that killed other people. To get where God wants you to go, you may have to go through this level of the Refiner's Fire. Trust me though, it will be worth it.

So let me give you a heads up. Going to deeper levels and desiring more of God no matter where you are in your walk always has what I call a spiritual backlash. It doesn't matter if you have been walking with Jesus a long time and you aren't tired yet or if you are brand new to Jesus and are just beginning your walk with God. Satan and his demonic forces want you either physically or spiritually dead (many times it's BOTH). Serving in a praise and worship ministry (or any sort of ministry) is an arduous journey that God has prepared for you if you choose to accept it. Depending on the road God needs you to go through, He will either make the way straight to deliver you from pain or He will allow you to walk the broken road and give you supernatural strength to overcome if you don't lose hope or faith. God always gives us a means to succeed and sometimes it's with a few scars and bruises. That's just real talk and we all need to hear it.

Often we don't want to hear "real talk" when it involves something that we need to change or alter in our lives. We don't want to look at reality when it involves uncovering our uncomely parts. We want to stay oblivious to the potential collateral damage that comes from being in a spiritual war. Make no mistake, the more you know about what's happening, the more serious our commitments to Christ become. Once we are immersed into the knowledge of who we are in Christ, a transformation occurs that causes us to see more and hear more from spiritual forces, whether or not we accept it. The truth may be a shock and hurt, but it is necessary.

I'm not trying to scare you, but I am trying to prepare you. I didn't have any warning and I had to discover many of these things, mostly on my own. God showed me the way even when I didn't see Him. God held my hand when I felt alone. I was isolated and felt abandoned. Little did I realize I needed to be put in a solitary place in order to be made over again in the image God had designed for me to have. I'm a man of science and, by my training, I don't usually believe in what I can't see without evidence. Logical thinking and self-reliance is a founding principle of my life. Being methodical and logical is the way my mind works. God had to shatter my reality and bring me not only to my knees, but He brought me to my face. I knew I wanted to serve Him in ministry, and I didn't know that I had to be stripped down to the ground and rebuilt. God provided me with the evidence I needed to be convinced that His awesome power is REAL!

Consecration does this most of the time. This is a journey of spiritual self-discovery and God discovery. God will guide us on not just one journey, but many journeys deep inside of His Heart if we desire it. He will whip us and correct us in such a way that even though it may hurt, it will soothe your spirit. God calls out to us, and we have to answer it if we want more. Once you taste the sweetness that is God's Presence, you always want more and more. It's an addiction that I never want to cure. The more we taste of Him, the more we desire Him, and God never enslaves us but empowers us. Yes, Satan will try to stop you, but if you keep your hand in God's Hand you won't fail. It might hurt and it will cost you, but God's rewards are always greater. Believe me. I also want to point out that this is a never-ending process. Time and time again you will be placed in the Fire to be purified.

For many of you reading this, it may be your first time delving into a spiritual journey. Even though every person has a unique experience, the goal is still the same: More of God. So no matter where you are in your walk with God, pursuing a deeper level in His Spirit should always be your goal. Anything that is stagnant and doesn't move or grow is dead. Many people get comfortable in ministry because they have overcome a few things and God uses them greatly and that is satisfactory to them. That is a deception from Hell. When we get comfortable, the Adversary adapts to our status quo.

When we stop moving, Satan doesn't stop. He fills in every blind spot and every shadow. The Enemy wants us to get complacent. That's why we should never sit still.

We should never think that our journey is at a peak or that we have reached an "enlightenment" until God reveals that to us we have gone as far as He has desired for us to go. When Paul knew his life was nearly over, he called his life a race and that he had finished his course (II Timothy 4:7). Doesn't that seem odd? A race speaks of running from a starting line to a finish line. A course is a planned route. To win any race, a competitor has to start where the organizer says to start and stay on the path for it to count. God is that organizer, and He has laid it all out for us. That alone is simply amazing!

So, back to this consecration thing. We've gone over the definition, the purpose, and the consequences. Having a definition is fine, but it requires the action of submission to actually achieve it. This action has to be made up in the mind, reconciled in the heart, agreed to by the spirit and executed via the flesh. So, after all of that, what do we do? We have to prepare for what is at hand. We need to get ready for the journey and to do that, we need to know what's ahead and how to overcome the challenges. Scripture gives us all the tools we need and how we are to put them into action. The same tools we spoke of before (fasting, prayer, scripture, and worship) are the proven methods we will need to use.

As I said earlier, I was inspired to write this book because the team I'm working with at the time of this writing (the Judah Worship Ministry) was preparing for a special Morning of Worship. Most of them had never participated in such an event and it broke new ground in that church and the community. We were seeking a significant move of God so that He would be glorified, and that people would receive healing and deliverance and touch the Heart of God. We wanted to lead people to that Secret Place in God that wants us all to go, and we had to prepare for what was coming. Satan didn't want this to happen, and he fought us all to prevent it. So we girded up our loins and got ready to charge into battle.

I've been where they are before and as a leader trying to do my best to lead people as God guides me I know they must be ready for not just the event and its setlist, but what will happen before the event and even while it's happening. I see their desire and I see the anointing in their lives, and I know God has destined them all for great things. This time together is just one short leg of a long journey in worship ministry. Their spiritual growth is happening, and they are asking God for more of what it takes. When we seek God, we will find Him (Matthew 7:7).

I can tell you with certainty that this Team has been under siege, and they know it will never stop. I taught them that it will never stop. Many have lost loved ones; some have experienced forced changes in their lives. Some have had to contend with critical concerns within their families. Some have endured sickness of themselves or their loved ones. You name it and this Team has been through it. I know that I've suffered loss too, like when I lost my father in 2020 or years back when my first marriage crumbled. What I have learned and what I have taught them is that losses in the natural realm will lead to windfalls in the spiritual realm. God's Eyes are not blind and if you are truly serving Him, He won't forget your sacrifices. He remembers every tear that was shed.

Whatever your reasoning for Consecration what is universal is that you are ready to have or a have a hunger for more of Him. Just remember that you will be rewarded for your journey ahead. We have to stay hungry and stay thirsty for God at all costs. When we have such a strong desire for Him, God reaches out to us to lead the way. Throughout scripture, we see people on different journeys from Moses to the Apostle Paul. Even though our flesh will fight us and will be under attack, our spirits will be empowered and awakened to the power of God like never before.

What we see when we reach that new level is up to God, but for me and many others, it is mind-blowing. Every time God takes us on a journey, He takes us higher. It's like the sun rising after being adrift at night on a storm-tossed sea. After a long and painful night of not being able to see where you were. Imagine being led only by a familiar voice in the dark, bidding you to keep going. You may trip over a few things and even stumble, but you keep going. Fear may try to paralyze you, but you don't totally lose hope. Just when you least expect it, the darkness rolls away and now here comes the sun as the night is over. You remember how many times you wanted to let go. You recall when your strength was gone that voice in your spirit calmly encouraged you. It reassured you and you felt safe amid certain danger. Sometimes there was no voice at all for a while. Your faith stretched to its limits and then (for now) this journey is over.

You will look back and wonder, *"How did I make it? How did I survive this?"* Then you realize God was there the whole time and He will let you know that He never left you (Jeremiah 23:39). He was always there with His eyes on you (Luke 12:6-7). He was there for you while you were going through it all (Isaiah 41:10). He loves you so much that He fought the battles for you that you didn't or couldn't see (Isaiah 45:2). He gave you the supernatural strength that you needed to endure all the pain (Psalms 46:1). He already had the plan in place to restore to you what was lost (Joel 1:4). God gave you rest for the tiredness (Exodus 33:14). He always gives us beauty for our ashes (Isaiah 61:3). He restores our souls (Psalms 23:3). He brings water and life back to our former desert places (Isaiah 43:19). He will heal what was injured or cut open to bleed (Psalms 147:3).

Yes, God can choose to use anyone and anything, but offering ourselves to be consecrated for His Glory and His use is "next level" stuff. Embrace it and God will open things up to you that you can't imagine. The moment we submit to being remade into what God wants us to be starts a process that only God can perform. To serve in ministry can be glorious as well as painful. There is a cost that we pay with our lives, but God is the greatest reward we could ever ask for. Just remember, the more we submit to God, the more He does for us and many times, the greater the reward. Being set apart means that you will be misunderstood and lonely. Sometimes only you and God truly understand what's happening. It's all still a part of God's Master Plan.

I don't want any of you reading this to think that God loves to torture us and that is far from the truth. God only wants the very best for us and He desires for us to be in relationship with Him on a deeper level. When we answer the call of ministry, it is important to know that being repurposed for God's use means that we have to suffer as Christ suffered for us. Look at how the Apostles ended up. Look at how they were close to Jesus and (except for Paul) walked and talked with Him. What they did, they didn't do for power or glory, but they did it for God. They knew what we know now after being saved, which is this is not our home. We live here right now, as real as it gets, but this is not our last stop. Eternity waits and for us to get there, we have to live on this Earth. We all know the stories of how we got here, but now we have to focus on the "ever after" and to do that, we have to be set apart, prepared, purified and sanctified for God's use.

PREPARATION

This chapter is just some general ideas on how to prepare for thirty days of consecration and deepening your walk with God. This isn't ceremonial, but this is a general guide if you aren't sure of what to do. Believe me when I tell you I learned all of this on the fly and from others that I am connected to. What I honestly suggest is that you take these ideas and make them work for your own personal journey. As long as you get to a deeper level in God, do what you have to do, but don't take the work for granted. It is still work!

Just like anything, you have to be ready for what comes next. Some of these things require physical sacrifices, so be sure to operate at a level that doesn't harm you, but will allow you to connect to God. I will explain what I mean in the following seven steps. Frankly, you also have to have some expectations of what you want to receive from God as well. You will have to mentally, physically and emotionally to get ready for what God will have in store for you and if you are truly seeking Him with all of your heart, you will find what you are looking for (Matthew 7:7).

As with any spiritual journey, God can change the scope because of the path that He has set for you. Either way, doing something consistently for over twenty-one days becomes a new habit and can tame the flesh and empower your spirit. Suppressing the human part of us allows us to release our spirits to God so we learn and grow with God. God will keep expanding your spiritual territory as far and as wide as your hunger and thirst. Just remember that. Take these steps with much prayer and meditation and let God lead you where you need to go and what He wants to say. I know it seems spooky, but it is what it is, and don't be afraid of what comes next.

Step 1: A Quiet Place

To get started, I think that it's best to find a quiet space where you can pray and meditate on God. This can be anything. A bedroom, a closet, a spare office at work, a place in the woods, or even in your car during a drive. It doesn't matter where or how, but find a place to separate yourself from everyone else. A place where you can turn your phone on silent, avoid TV or social media. A place that gives your mind peace and is not necessarily comfortable, but that depends on you. For me, creature comforts make me lazy and will lull me to sleep or to drift away from my motivation.

Find a place where you can get focused and not be distracted. This is important. We need a space that we can be unashamed in a human sense. We need a place where we can let loose and be open and spiritually naked before God (not physically naked, so please don't think you need to strip down to your birthday suit, ok?) and open up our souls and spirits to Him. Our humanity feels more at ease when we feel like no one is watching or can hear us. We can be more genuine or free when we are going into an undiscovered country.

Isolation is critical because the Adversary uses our five human senses to keep us occupied from spiritual concerns. It's also necessary to let people know that this is your quiet place. If it is in an area that you can control, like your home, you may have to post a little sign or let people know you aren't to be disturbed (be nice and kind about it) and that you need this time. Remember, the best support can sometimes be your family if they understand getting closer to God. However, if they don't and you are alone, use your best judgement and ask God for wisdom for what you need to do. If it is somewhere you can't control scope out the place and observe how and when people come in or out or if there are environmental concerns like a natural phenomenon or anything that could disturb your peace like the noise of traffic or blasts from sirens. I know it feels extreme, but trust me, it is well worth it.

Step 2: A Space of Time

What good is having a quiet place when you don't make the time? Many things to kill off every waking moment we have available have occupied our lives in this world. Work, school, social activities, relationships, and even (gasp!) the church itself. We as humans are always "running out of time" because we have so much on our plates. It seems that way because of how we perceive time. Time flies when we're having fun and if we're really honest, we use a lot of time in leisure activities.

We sometimes don't realize how much time we actually waste during the day and once we "discover" what we waste, it will surprise us. Take the time to map out your day and write on paper what you do and how much time you take to do it. If you can keep a time diary for a day or two and see how it goes. I know it's a lot, but it pays dividends to your life and not just in this Consecration.

The key to any relationship is time. What we give our time to is what will ultimately feed and grow us. When we give up time for things we like to do and give them to God, it reaps benefits. I know it seems insane that if we mere mortals give an eternal God (who is beyond time) our personal time, He will reward us greatly. It just makes little sense from a human perspective, but every sacrifice we make for God, He takes notice. Remember that simple point... Every sacrifice. This time with the Lord isn't just any old appointment on our calendars. We have to GIVE UP SOMETHING that we want for it to be considered a sacrifice. We may have to give up our favorite TV show or recreational activity. Maybe it's that extra nap after dinner that we just do because we have nothing else slated. Whatever it is, it has to be something that is premium to us and our flesh. Abel gave a sacrificial offering to God while Cain gave God something left over. We all should know the story... Cain's offering was rejected. We must give our best up for God. I know it's tough. I know it will hurt, but it is totally necessary. No exceptions.

Step 3: Prayer

Now that we have the place and the time, we need to make the first move. We need to talk to God. We need to open up the hailing frequencies and bombard Heaven like we may never have before. Prayer is communication with God on a physical and spiritual level. It can be anything from daily prayer, intercessory prayer, petitioning God for deliverance, prayers in the midnight hour, prayers for supplication, and many, many more. For every type of request, there is a way to pray for it. Mind you, this isn't formal. What we need to accomplish here is a consistent connection to God and at first, it will seem unusual. It will seem like it "isn't working" and our humanity will think it's silly. Because of the Fall of Adam, communicating with God has been strange. Remember, once Adam sinned and God talked to Adam, he felt shame. He felt like he couldn't talk to God like he once did. If you don't have a powerful prayer life, it seems weird talking to God when you can't see Him. I know it's strange, but hang in there.

So many people and so many religions have made prayer more of a ritual than a means of communing with God. Yes, He is eternal and all-powerful and yes; He is infinite, but in all of this, He can hear your voice out of billions. We may not see Him, but He can see and hear us. He knows our names. He knows everything about us, and He waits for us to talk. He whispers to us and gives us signs He is there for us. The amazing thing is that we talk to Him, and God does TALK BACK TO US. It may or may not be in a human language. It could be an injection of thoughts, seeing confirmation in a text or on a billboard. Either way, you KNOW that it's God's Voice. It's called a conversation because it is one. The first person speaks, and the other person responds. It's no different. Why make a request or a declaration and not have a response? Right? We as people don't like a "one-sided" conversation and our God is full of wisdom and love so why not let Him speak to us?

One more thing that I cannot and won't overlook and that is repentance. I think it's a great thing to repent for sins of omission and commission and our lifestyles. That means sins we know about and sins that we don't realize we commit or have already committed. Just remember that repentance is more than just saying that you are sorry. Repentance is a commitment to shift away from what we did wrong into what we need to do right. In Chapter Five, we will have daily prayer time with a focus on that devotional, but always pray to get things right with God. Repentance isn't just for the unsaved, but for everyone who has stepped out of the ways of God, and it must be done continually.

Step 4: The Word of God

What journey into the Heart of God can be complete without His Word? There are many verses in scripture that detail being prepared for not just service in ministry but in relationship with God Himself. When we read the Bible, we shouldn't look at it as a simple literary collection of stories. The Word of God was given to humanity so that we can look back at how He has been over history as well as how things will be in the future. It's like a diary. It's a full spectrum account of just about everything we can experience in life. Ecclesiastes 1:9 (written by the great and wise King Solomon) said that there was nothing new under the sun. God is the same yesterday, today, and forever (Hebrews 13:8). God declared to us He never changes (Malachi 3:6). The Bible is God in written form (John 1:1). The one thing that separates God's Word from everything else? It is ALIVE!

When we read a human diary, we get to know the deepest thoughts and actions of people. We learn about them almost as we would talk to them. The Word is so powerful that it came in human form and lived with us. Any spiritual journey with God makes studying and digesting His Word a necessity. In His Word, there is life and power. The Bible may have been translated and abused by humanity over the years (that is a whole other conversation, but one you should look into), but with the Holy Spirit, Who is the great Teacher, there is nothing we cannot attain from Scripture. Nothing.

Here are just a few examples:

> ***Romans 12:1-2*** – *I beseech you therefore, brethren, by the mercies of God, that ye present your bodies a living sacrifice, holy, acceptable unto God, which is your*

reasonable service. And be not conformed to this world: but be ye transformed by the renewing of your mind, that ye may prove what is that good, and acceptable, and perfect, will of God.

I Peter 2:9 – *But ye are a chosen generation, a royal priesthood, a holy nation, a peculiar people; that ye should shew forth the praises of him who hath called you out of darkness into His marvelous light:*

I Corinthians 6:20 – *For ye are bought with a price: therefore glorify God in your body, and in your spirit, which are God's.*

II Timothy 2:20-21 – *But in a great house there are not only vessels of gold and of silver, but also of wood and of earth; and some to honor, and some to dishonor. If a man, therefore, purge himself from these, he shall be a vessel unto honor, sanctified, and meet for the Master's use, and prepared unto every good work.*

Psalms 51:17 – *The sacrifices of God are a broken spirit: a broken and a contrite heart, O God, thou wilt not despise.*

II Corinthians 8:5 – *And this they did, not as we hoped, but first gave their own selves to the Lord, and unto us by the will of God.*

Romans 6:13 – *Neither yield ye your members as instruments of unrighteousness unto sin: but yield yourselves unto God, as those that are alive from the dead, and your members as instruments of righteousness unto God.*

Romans 6:16 – *Know ye not, that to whom ye yield yourselves servants to obey, His servants ye are to whom ye obey; whether of sin unto death, or of obedience unto righteousness?*

33

Romans 6:19 *– I speak after the manner of men because of the infirmity of your flesh: for as ye have yielded your members servants to uncleanness and to iniquity unto iniquity; even so now yield your members servants to righteousness unto holiness.*

Isaiah 44:3 *– For I will pour water upon him that is thirsty, and floods upon the dry ground: I will pour my Spirit upon thy seed, and my blessing upon thine offspring:*

Joshua 3:5 *– Then Joshua said to the people, "Consecrate yourselves, for tomorrow the Lord will do wonders among you."*

Isaiah 41:10 *– Fear thou not; for I am with thee: be not dismayed; for I am thy God: I will strengthen thee; yea, I will help thee; yea, I will uphold thee with the right hand of my righteousness.*

There are many more verses in the Bible, but I've only listed a few here for your reference, and I suggest you add your own favorites and find new ones that you need. The Word is dynamic and living, so let God direct you to where He wants you to go. Believe me, He will and will always guide us. One more chapter I'd recommend is Hebrews, Chapter 12. A great reminder of what God has done through the faith His people have had over the many ages!

Step 5: Worship

What's a worshipper's journey into the Heart of God without worship? For some, this may be difficult because they rarely worship alone, but I highly recommend that you do in this Consecration and outside of it. Since you have a place and time set aside, it's important to dive into the Presence of God. Since you are or will be alone while you worship, you can let loose and not worry about onlookers or eavesdroppers. You can be your authentic self and you can go in deep whenever you want to and however you want to take the plunge.

Worship itself has been misconceived by many for a very long time. We often ask God to "visit us" or "stop by here for a little while" and the imagery makes us relate to a God way up high in the heavens visiting us on Earth. It is actually the other way around. Psalms 24:3-4 asks us, "*Who may ascend into the hill of the Lord? And who may stand in His holy place? He who has clean hands and a pure heart, who has not lifted up his soul to falsehood and has not sworn deceitfully."* I love this passage because it clearly illustrates not only the method but the prerequisites to be in God's Presence. We have to ascend or rise upward to get there. We are on Earth. God is everywhere, but His Throne is ON HIGH. God is Spirit and we worship Him in Spirit and in truth (John 4:24). God doesn't have to move. We do. We must spiritually reach His heights to overcome our ground-centered flesh and the biggest question I get all the time is how do we do it?

Well, just in case you don't know the model of worship, I will explain it how I teach it to my teams. I call it the Psalms 100 Model and perhaps it can help you too. Let's start with verse 1 of the psalm, which is how we start worship. With a joyful noise (Psalms 100:1). Bless the Lord with your lips. Open your mouth and speak out words of gratitude and thanks for what God is to you. Tell Him how marvelous and wonderful He is. Clap your hands and be glad for He is our God and Savior! Have happiness and joy in your heart and break out into a song of praise if you know one or make one up (Psalms 100:2) because there are no rules here.

Affirm that He is God, and He is the One who made us because we couldn't and no one else could either. We are His people and the sheep of His pasture (Psalms 100:3). Tell God how these things make you feel. Let it all out and don't be afraid to say it aloud. Why aloud? Because the Adversary hates the praises to our God. Praise is a weapon and Hell can't stand it and must leave the premises. Turn whatever place you are in into a temple unto The Lord. Be intentional and be persistent. You may start to feel foolish or even feel sick. Keep pressing and don't stop. It will be worth it.

Here is where the model gets interesting. The Temple of God that Solomon built was designed a certain way based on the Tabernacle of the Wilderness. There were five components of the structure: the pair of columns at the entrance or "gate" (Jachin and Boaz), the Forecourt or "Outer Court" (Ulam), the Outer Sanctum or the "Inner Court" (Hechal), the Holy of Holies (Devir), and the side chamber (Yatsia Sovev)[4]. For the sake of the Psalms 100 model, we will exclude (even though it is important, and you should look it up) the side chamber.

Verse 4 of Psalms 100 says to *"enter into His gates with thanksgiving"* which is what you did first. Thanking God. The same verse continues with *"and into His courts with praise"* and this is where it gets deeper. When we bless God for what He has done, something changes. Our praise turns from what God has done (Outer Court) into thanking God for who He is (Inner Court). Then the verse continues as we travel into the Inner Court you begin to *"be thankful unto him, and bless his name"* and if you don't know His Name

---

[4] Garfinkel, Y, & Mumcuoglu, M. (2019, March 15). *The Temple of Solomon in Iron Age Context*. Religions. https://www.mdpi.com/2077-1444/10/3/198/htm

here are a few examples:

1. He is The LORD *(Adonai)* — Psalms 8; Isaiah 40:3-5; Ezekiel 16:8; Habakkuk 3:19
2. He is God Alone *(Yahweh)* — Exodus 3:14; Malachi 3:6
3. He is God Almighty **(El-Shaddai)** — Genesis 17:1-3; 35:11; 48:3; 49:25 Psalms 90:2
4. He is the Ancient of Days *(Attiq Yomin)* — Daniel 7:9, 13, 22
5. He is the Everlasting God *(El Olam)* — Psalms 90:1-2; Isaiah 40:28; Romans 1:20
6. He is the Living God *(Elohim Chayim)* — Jeremiah 10:10
7. He is the Lord Creator *(Elohim, Jehovah-Bore)* — Genesis 1:1-3; Psalms 68; Mark 13:19
8. He is the Lord of Hosts *(Jehovah-Sabaoth)* — Malachi 1:10-14; Romans 9:29
9. He is our Provider *(Jehovah-Jireh)* — Genesis 22:13-14 Psalms 23:1
10. He is our Healer *(Jehovah-Rapha)* — Exodus 15:25-27; Psalms 103:3; 147:3; I Peter 2:24
11. He is our Peace *(Jehovah-Shalom)* — Numbers 6:26; Isaiah 9:6; Hebrews 13:20
12. He is our Righteousness *(Jehovah-Tsidkenu)* — Jeremiah 23:5-6; II Corinthians 5:21
13. He is our Sanctification *(Adonai Mekaddishkem)* — Leviticus 20:8; Ezekiel 20:12
14. He is our Shepherd *(Jehovah-Rohi)* — Psalms 23; Isaiah 53:6; Revelation 7:17
15. He is our Banner *(Jehovah-Nissi)* — Exodus 17:15-16; Isaiah 11:10-12
16. He is our Protector *(Jehovah-Magen)* — Genesis 15:1; Ephesians 6:16; Psalms 91:4
17. He is our Rock *(Jehovah-Selah)* — Psalms 18:2; I Corinthians 10:4; 1; Matthew 16:18
18. He is our Strength *(Jehovah-Kjail)* — Habakkuk 3:1 Exodus 15:2; Philippians 4:13
19. He is always present *(Jehovah-Shammah)* — Ezekiel 48:35; Psalms 46; Matthew 28:20
20. He is Jesus Christ, Son of the LIVING GOD! *(Yeshu'a Ha-Mashiach)* – Matthew 16:16; Mark 8:29; Luke 9:20

At this point, our spirit takes over and the flesh will fade away into the back seat. We can't utter these sorts of things from our heart, and something will not happen. The surrounding atmosphere will shift, and we will meet the

Presence of God beyond the veil of the Holy of Holies where He Himself will sing (or speak) over us (Zephaniah 3:17-19) and minister back to us. Whether or not you have music playing in the background, it really doesn't matter. If you want to enter into His Presence and enter sweet communion with God, it WILL HAPPEN. Keep going until something happens. Keep the faith until God starts to move. You can't do this wrong, and you can't mess this up. Just press into God and He will press into you.

Step 6: Fasting

Some people are afraid of this activity because it is very misunderstood. Let me be clear about what I believe as it relates to fasting. Fasting can be from food like skipping a meal to pray. Some people can abstain from food or even drink for several days and not miss a beat. Many people can't do that because of many factors such as personal health issues like hypoglycemia, diabetes or other health conditions. Some people have medication or regiment needs you need to perform in order to survive. Don't worry, it is okay, and you should do what you can for your situation. I would advise that if you have a health concern and you want to fast from food or drink, consult your doctor and find out what's best for you. Different food fasts include all-day fasts, sunrise-sunset fasting, single meal or giving up a certain food that you really love and enjoy. Whatever you do, it has to be a sacrifice to deny your flesh, but do it safely. God knows your heart.

Other types of fasts include not doing certain activities that you enjoy such as watching TV, time on social media, playing video games or (for married people) abstaining from sexual activities (BTW, if you're having sex you should be married and only having sex with the person you married and I so wish I didn't have to clarify that, but anyway) or any other type of sacrifice that denies your flesh. For those who are giving up sex, be sure that your spouse agrees with you (I Corinthians 7:5) and if not, you're going to have to pick something else to give up. Sorry... Now before the married people out there please don't freak out and don't send hate mail. Your bedroom life can and will return to normal after the agreed hiatus is over. Just be willing to work with your spouse and help them through their journey IF that's what they gave up.

There is another category of sacrifices that is for many a hard pill to swallow and that pill is the one of your addictions. Not all addictions are mortally harmful, although they are perfect candidates for allowing God to help you beat them in order to help your body. What I am talking about are the things that border on obsession. For example, I think that working out and fitness are great, but if they are taking up so much time that you can't have any for God? Consider changing that routine. Another one of these areas is controversial and that is the people who are addicted to church and I'm already ducking from the things that might be thrown at me.

Sometimes that weekly grind of church activities can also actually keep you from deep communion with God. I said what I said. I didn't say that they were bad because attending bible studies, choir rehearsals and organizational meetings are (most times) positive things, but consider this viewpoint. There are people who went from being addicted to substances to being addicted to church. There are people who spend more time at church than at home with their families. God loves for us to be together with the other church people, but He wants time alone with us, too. Think about your significant other for a second. If you went and did things with them as well as other people all the time, is it good that you spend that time together? YES, but what time do you have with them intimately and alone? How many human relationships would last like that?

Fasting brings about discipline, because taming the flesh empowers the spirit within us. Consecration is not a normal thing to our human realm, and we need to get ourselves under control. Some people find that after giving up something during a fast that they learn to live without them, and it makes their lives better. Let that be between you and God on what you decide.

Step 7: Keep a Journal

Journaling is a good way to record the dreams, visions, words of knowledge, and confirmations from God. Keeping a personal record of not just this spiritual journey, but in the future keeping a record of these things can help remind you of what God said or did when you may need it in a time of trouble or if you are sharing with someone else who may embark on their journey. Journals are also a great way to track the promises of God and the progress being made in the human realm towards their completion.

You will want to jot down the things you experience because our memory can be faulty and what we share today may be for some time in the future. Remember, God is beyond time and what He reveals is for whatever time He decides. Writing things down just helps us to remember events as they freshly happen to us and trust me, one day you will want to remember. Nothing is too small or great when it comes to revelations from God. God doesn't believe in fluff and unnecessary details, and He is a "straight shooter", and He is as real as it gets.

This journal doesn't have to be formal, and it doesn't have to be something that you have to share with anyone unless you are led to do so. Don't feel pressure to make it "perfect", but make it so that you can decipher it and go back to it when you need it. Keep it by our bedside or take it with you when you leave home and have it ready wherever you may be. God doesn't work on a set schedule to reveal things to you, so always be ready. It will be a vital resource to you!

THIRTY DAYS OF DEVOTIONALS

When I was inspired to write this book, I felt I was led to divide the thirty days into themes to help people new to consecration make some sense of it all. It can be intimidating going into the unknown and for me it was a humbling experience. It makes you fearful and uncertain and believe it or not that gives the Adversary a way to stop you. Fear is a powerful motivator to quit. Fear is like gravity, as it desires to keep us where we currently are. Faith empowers us to move forward and upward. A journey or process requires effort or transformation. These words and these activities are defined by change.

Anything that doesn't move, grow, or change is dead. We have a lot of Christians who are moving mainly in the flesh while earning many accomplishments and accolades and are numb in their spirits. Many can sing like the sweetest of angels and can move emotions and lift spirits. Many can preach the paint off of the walls of the sanctuary with fervor and might. Many can play instruments with the skill and precision of a surgeon and yet are still dead inside. They are writing books, releasing albums, and even appearing on TV and social media and they are spiritually DECEASED.

Why, you may ask? Because of the trap of religion. Religion (especially organized religion) can be, and many times is a literal cancer within the Body of Christ (YES, I said it). Religion is a human process of how we relate to God and what we should strive and live for is a relationship with God. A relationship is a living and breathing thing that we have to feed for it to survive (as we discussed earlier) and what this series of devotionals are designed to do is work on specific points that will grow us in Christ especially if you are a worship leader. I pray that after each day you will receive insights and revelation from God what you have to do to move closer and closer to

Him. It will take some time and devoting this time to God is definitely worth it.

Some people believe (and some don't) that it takes (at the minimum) about twenty-one days to be devoted to an activity in order for it to become a habit. Choosing an entire month or thirty days in order to enter consecration allows us to get into a routine of giving God daily time and devotion, and it also cements in us a new beginning and foundation for what God will lead us into in the future. It also tells our flesh that we took a chunk out of an entire year to devote ourselves to be reconditioned into something new.

When God inspired me to create these devotionals, one thing I asked God was *"Exactly how should this be done?"* After much prayer, I received some instruction and wrote what I heard. It seems a little different at first, but God showed me how this would all come together. So, here is how I've divided up the days for this Consecration:

- Part I: God, I Need You
- Part II: God, I Adore You
- Part III: God, Show Me Who I Am
- Part IV: God, Prepare Me
- Part V: God, Teach Me
- Part VI: God I, Am Yours
- Part VII: God, I Thank You

Before you begin I want to agree with you in prayer that you will attain what you are looking for from God. I touch and agree with you in the Name of Jesus that no devil will stop you and that every assignment of Hell is cancelled that has been placed on your life. IAs I write this I pray that you as you read this will receive the strength you need to endure these thirty days of devotionals and that your faith will not fail you and that you will plunge into God like you never have before. I am also praying that you will receive powerful revelations from God and that He speaks to you clearly and often to breathe a new life into your spirit. I declare and decree it to be so in the Name of Jesus and sealed by the Blood of the Lamb!

Don't forget to make sure that you take the lessons from Chapter Four as a framework and have everything ready to begin. Each one of those items is key critical to keeping yourself grounded and ready for what's about to happen. I suggest that you bookmark this place in the book so that you can easily get back to it again and again and a second bookmark for each day that you are currently reading. Are you ready? Take a deep breath, get into your quiet place and let's begin…

Part I: God, I Need You

Day 1: Hear My Cry, O God

Hear my cry, O God; attend unto my prayer. From the
end of the earth will I cry unto thee, when my heart is
overwhelmed: lead me to the rock that is higher than I. —
Psalms 61:1-2 KJV

Welcome to the first day! I pray you are truly ready and excited for what is coming on this journey into God's Heart. Today we humbly recognize and submit to our Righteous and Powerful God who is omnipotent and yet so close that He hears our prayer. Yes, the God of the Universe can hear when you call on Him! Even though billions may pray all at the same time, God can hear just your voice and respond.

I grew up on the old hymns of the church. Being a young little fellow, I didn't understand them as I do today. Those songs are the ones that I sang from my youth growing up in church, singing from whatever hymnal was available. I remember hearing the soaring voices singing with such passion and such reverence. The old hymn Pass Me Not, written by Fanny J. Crosby, is one of my favorites today and the lyrics of personal declaration and admiration for a mighty God still ring true today. One line of the song (I believe) is one of the most misunderstood lyrics of them all:

"While on others Thou art calling; do not pass me by!"

As I got older and wiser, I realized what the words really meant. In this Refrain the word "calling" wasn't what modern American English defines it as, which we know it as communication like a phone call between people. In older English, however, calling meant to visit someone or see about them socially. When I learned this now, I saw how powerful those words were. *"While on others Thou art calling"* now becomes "While You are visiting other people" don't pass me by. Don't forget about me God, because I'm still here! Don't ignore me because I'm crying out to You God! Lord, please visit me because I'm desperate, I'm in trouble and I have no choice but to call out to You. God, You are all I have and all I need and there is no One like You! The song calls out Savior! Savior! Hear my humble cry! The song speaks of submission, and it speaks of an urgent need. That, my friends is amazing!

God is so massive and yet so personal that it is a mystery why such a powerful God would even care about us. He made everything everywhere and He loves us beyond what we can measure. While God spoke everything into existence with every detail with the words *"Let there be..."* and it became so, He formed us from the dust of the ground with His own hands. He made it personal and intentional. Even though He said, *"Let Us make man in Our own Image"* God used His Hands to create us. He shaped our every detail. Everything operates and functions in Creation with precision. Every orbiting planet, each star in the heavens, the mix of gases in the atmosphere, and each fingerprint on every hand is uniquely different. That's power. That's huge. That's our God!

So as we begin this journey, let us cry out to God earnestly to hear us and to feel the depths of our hearts. We want to change our relationship with God from being ritualistic to being personal. We want a move of God in our lives like we have never seen before. We are seeking more of Him, and we want less of us. Our desire should be that God takes us over and uses us for His Glory. God reveals Himself to us in ways we have never experienced, and we want more revelation and more visitation from the Lord. We desire to submit to God and lay ourselves bare and unashamed before Him. This is why we are crying out. God, we want You and only You!

Know that He is listening to you. Like a parent who hears their baby crying from the next room, God will respond. I have heard mothers say that they learn to determine what a baby needs based on the type of cry that they hear, and God is no different. God knows the cries of His children and when we truly and honestly cry out to God, He responds to that cry. Sometimes He will come right away to where you are. Sometimes He will listen and work in the background. Sometimes He will wait because He wants to see something grow in you or change in you. No matter the response, God hears you and loves you and will do what's best for you. Make it personal. Make it count and make it loud! Let your heart explode with the desire for God to hear you. If you aren't convinced that you need God, why would He answer? He already knows that we need Him. He already knows that we are nothing without Him. He still knows and He waits for you. He wants you and loves you and that's more than enough to cry out to God!

So as you enter your prayer corner today, let the focus not be on the things we want. Don't ask for a single thing for yourself even if you are in need because he truly already knows. Our prayers should be direct and to the point... God, I need You. I need You now. I'm desperate for You and all I want is You. I don't know anyone else but You who can fulfill me. There is no One else who can rebuild me; no One else who can protect me! Our hearts should be overwhelmed with the desire for His perfect Presence. Today we humbly cry out for the Rock that's higher than us (Psalms 61:2)!

Day 2: IF, THEN, or ELSE

If my people, which are called by my name, shall humble themselves, and pray, and seek my face, and turn from their wicked ways; then will I hear from heaven, and will forgive their sin, and will heal their land. Now mine eyes shall be open, and mine ears attend unto the prayer that is made in this place. — II Chronicles 7:14-15 KJV

Welcome to Day 2! We know God is all-powerful and all-seeing and that He loves us. God has known us from the very beginning even before our beginning began. He knew us when the Garden of Eden was created, and He knew us when Christ suffered on the Cross of Calvary. As I have said many times before, God is a being beyond time and because of that He knows all that we were, is, and will be. It doesn't matter what we think about us, God already knows. Yet, Jesus paid our sin debt so that we would be made free. Let's be real… Who does that?

God hears us every time we pray, and we can rest assured that He will not only hear, but answer in His time. Still, the verse for today gave us some "conditions" for God to not only hear but respond. The word "if" is an enormous word with two letters. "If" is a conditional statement. When I went to college, I studied Computer Science and we had to learn how to program as a part of understanding how computers worked. Programs use different scenarios in order to run and perform functions. In the computer programming world, an IF statement evaluates a certain defined condition in order to start whatever process will follow and is followed by a THEN statement which tells what must be done and, most times how long to do it. If there was more than one desired outcome, there was an ELSE statement that did something that the THEN statement didn't do. To simplify all of this in order to get the THEN, you have to pass the IF.

The scripture said that IF God's people who are called by His Name would SEEK HIS FACE and TURN FROM THEIR WICKED WAYS… THEN… Let's stop here for a second. Each one of you that is called to ministry by God or has accepted Jesus as your Lord and Savior are indeed God's people. Besides all of that, you are on this journey into the Heart of God, and you are looking for Him more deeply. You are seeking His Face. So congratulations, you have met the first part of the requirements, but there are more things to do.

Here is where we have some decisions to make. We have to turn from our wicked ways. Now stop and let's not overreact here. I'm not saying that you are wicked, but the verse states that some of God's people have wicked ways. This isn't a call out, but a chance for us to examine ourselves. God knows everything about you, including those things you hide from others. Those secret things we do that don't please God. We know what they are, and He does, too. He sees them and still lets us keep breathing when we really don't deserve it. He knows who and what we are, and God still gives us the time to make it right.

After self-examination, we have to turn from those things in our lives that we already know don't please God. We have to abandon behaviors that separate us from God and go in a more Godly direction. We can't keep doing what we were doing. We have to ask for forgiveness and repent of the sins that we commit or practice regularly. Why is this important? Because of THEN… Not meeting the conditions stated earlier after the IF breaks our end of the promise. God said THEN He will hear from Heaven. THEN He will forgive their sin and heal their land. Meet the requirements and then get the results. What isn't stated in the verse is what can be implied. IF God's people don't do as God asked, then the ELSE comes into play. The ELSE are the consequences God has laid out for us whatever they might be. God hears those prayers and won't act because we didn't hold up our end of the bargain. God made it plain and His Word yet again gives us clear and plain direction.

So as you enter your prayer corner today, it is time to be honest with yourself and honest with God. We have to beg for God's forgiveness for the sin in our lives. All of it. You know what they are. You're thinking about it right now. It's time to come clean and fess up to what we have done wrong. Like a parent knows what their child did all God wants is an honest confession. The beauty of all of this is God won't chew you out for what you confess. Those sins have already been paid for. He just wants us to come clean with Him and ourselves. Lay it all out before Him and tell God that you're sorry. That you will repent or turn from your wicked ways and MEAN IT. Even those minor sins can ruin us. Let's cast our cares upon God and let Him heal our land. God is waiting for us so that He can lay His Hands on our lives and heal them, but we have to do what He asks us first. Otherwise, we will live the ELSE by our reluctance to fulfill the IF.

Day 3: I Can't Do This Without You

Abide in me, and I in you. As the branch cannot bear fruit of itself, except it abide in the vine; no more can ye, except ye abide in me. I am the vine, ye are the branches: He that abideth in me, and I in him, the same bringeth forth much fruit: for without me ye can do nothing. — *John 15:4-5*
KJV

Welcome to Day 3! I pray that by now God has opened up to you as He has turned His Face towards you after crying out to Him asking for His love and His grace. It is a very humbling thing for us to fall on our faces and admit that we are but tiny specks in this universe and that a God that we cannot see with our eyes is in control of everything and even our existence. It's a scary thought, but reassuring at the same time.

It seems unreal that God would even care about us. What real reason would He truly love us? We, humans were given everything in Eden. We didn't have to earn money and there was no war or disease. We were made to live forever in direct communication with God. He laid it all out for us and even gave us a purpose in tending the Garden. It's like a child growing up in our household. They don't have to worry about any actual issues. They get fed; they get clothed, and they are protected from danger. Who wouldn't want that? All God asked is that we leave one tree alone and not even touch it. Nope, we listened to the serpent and believed someone who wasn't God and betrayed Him. We sinned.

Growing up, I remember my grandmother had a saying where she would quip when people weren't doing right and she would say *"I'm so glad I'm not God because I wouldn't put up with these people!"* It really makes me think now that I am older and somewhat wiser that God has a ton of patience with us and it's mind-blowing. How can He be so loving and calm with us when we mess things up so badly? Why does He continue to bless us when He should slam the door in our faces? It's hard for us to realize that we cannot do anything without Him. We can't breathe, move, or exist without God. It makes us feel small and it really should when we think about it.

We are insignificant specks of dust compared to the whole of Creation. Our star Sol (we call it the Sun) is one of billions of stars in one of billions of galaxies in a universe that is still expanding since God said, *"Let there be…"* and it was. Our home, the Earth, is one of eight planets (sorry Pluto) that can support life. Each human is one of over 7 billion souls living on the Earth. We have zero control over anything. We breathe without thinking about it. Our heart beats without our command. We don't move food through our bodies to nourish us. Here's the relief... God is in control of it all. Every single thing God has orchestrated with masterful precision and without Him, we are nothing. All of this because God willed it to be so.

A single piece of metal hurled from a gun can kill us. The water on the Earth that gives us life can also rise and drown us. A single meteor can crash into our planet and snuff out all life. Our very Sun could explode and kill every living thing on this planet in mere seconds. The black hole that is at the center of our galaxy could suck us all in and crush us to death. Dangers seen and unseen are all around us and the same God we defy and disobey still knows our name. He still loves us. He still provides for us. He protects us with His Mighty Hand. If God desired it, we would blink out of existence. Our existence is meaningless, and He calls us His friend.

So as you enter your prayer corner today, pour out your gratitude to our God for all that He is to you. Let Him know you can't do this life without Him. Let God see the tears in your eyes. Let Him witness your realization that you are tiny and insignificant by any other measure, but His. Pray for more understanding of how He works in you and around you. Ask God for the humility that comes with being His son or daughter. Shower God with your adoration and your love for Him. Don't limit yourself and after a while let your spirit take over. Let it speak to God. Let whatever comes out of your mouth flow. Let your heart and soul be emptied into God so that He can fill you up. How deeply we need Him. How little He needs us, but still He loves us!

Part II: God I Adore You

Day 4: Oh, How I Love Jesus

That at the name of Jesus every knee should bow, of things in heaven, and things in earth, and things under the earth; And that every tongue should confess that Jesus Christ is Lord, to the glory of God the Father. Wherefore, my beloved, as ye have always obeyed, not as in my presence only, but now much more in my absence, work out your own salvation with fear and trembling. — Philippians 2:10-12 KJV

Welcome to Day 4! For the last three days, we have been telling God how much we need Him and how we cannot go through life without Him. How can we not shower our love upon God, who is everything to us? Once we see the Hand of God with our senses, we can't help but desire the Heart of God that has been, is, and will always be for us and never against us. He did all He has done, doing and will do for us and when we see these things and how selfless He has been, it should cause us to love God because He loved us first.

Just imagine if God had our limitations. Picture how salvation would have been impossible with any other sort of love. God's love has no depth that we can measure and no limit we can see. His love is amazing and powerful and when we recognize that love it causes our hearts to burn for God like no one else. It changes our outlook on life and transforms how we once were into what Christ desires for us to be. Embracing the love of Jesus is overwhelming and beautiful. He gave His life for ours. It's a truly beautiful exchange!

I love new worship music and I love the atmosphere that gets cleaned when powerful worship goes forth. The old church way back in the day, however, didn't have the fancy music we have today, but the songs they had had some of the most powerful words ever written and sung. One of the old hymns of the church that I remember well *O, How I Love Jesus* is one of my favorites, and the verses were written by a man named Frederick Whitfield. They say that the song was based on today's scripture, and it truly shows. He wrote these beautiful words:

There is a name I love to hear,
I love to sing its worth.
It sounds like music in my ear,
The sweetest name on earth.

It tells me of a Savior's love,
Who died to set me free.
It tells me of His precious blood,
The sinner's perfect plea.

It tells of One whose loving heart
Can feel my deepest woe.
Who in each sorrow bears a part
That none can bear below.

It is the Refrain of this hymn that many of us are familiar with, and we don't truly know who wrote it, but it goes like this:

O how I love Jesus,
O how I love Jesus,
O how I love Jesus,
Because He first loved me!

God loves us and it shows. In our relationships, we always look for evidence that we are loved. The little things count. God shows us daily and all around us and yet, sadly many will refuse to see that love. We have the opportunity to profess our love for Jesus openly and willingly. This is us returning beauty for beauty. God loves us openly and we should do the same. This love also means that we should show that love to others even when they may not deserve it.

Love opens doors and makes a way out of no way. When we truly experience and understand the love of God, our lives are never the same. It's infectious and that's a great thing. We as humans need to shower our God with love and adoration because He loved us when we in no way deserved His Love. God made the first move and He proved Himself with His actions. He showed His Love with Jesus dying on the cross. He stretched His arms wide and showed us He loved us "that much"! It is so lopsided how much He loves us and does for us, and we are so tiny and can't do nearly as much for Him. Realizing how deep His Love is for us should make our hearts burn with an unquenchable fire for Him!

So, as you enter your prayer corner today, tell God just how much you love Him. Profess your love for God like you never have before. Thank Him and bless Him for all that He has done and who He is. Pour out the oil in your Alabaster Box and spare no details about how much you love Jesus. Because His love letter to us is everything in Creation. His sacrifice on the Cross showed us how far He would go to win us back. When we tap in and let our whole being pour out love on Jesus, something amazing happens. God opens up our eyes to how overwhelming His Love is. It causes a chain reaction of love that floods not just ourselves, but everyone around us. That's love in action. That love is unlimited and that's some powerful love!

Day 5: God's Love In Action

*But God commendeth his love toward us, in that, while
we were yet sinners, Christ died for us. Much more then,
being now justified by his blood, we shall be saved from
wrath through him. For if, when we were enemies, we
were reconciled to God by the death of his Son, much
more, being reconciled, we shall be saved by his life. —
Romans 5:8-10 KJV*

Welcome to Day 5! Our journey continues into the Heart of God and today we turn our focus towards the gift of salvation. I know that we have all gone over this again and again, but we, as Christians need to revisit it sometimes so that we remember how much God loves us. We've talked about God's Love Letter of Creation and all that He has done for us as evidence and now we look at that sequence of thirty-three years that Jesus came to Earth in human flesh and fulfilled a promise that was kept over forty-two generations to humanity that the error of sin would be corrected, and God and humanity would be reconciled. I sometimes think slowly about all of what God did for us.

From the moment Adam sinned, God had a plan for us. He knew that for us humans to believe what He did, God would have to do it on a big scale. We don't believe things until we see them. God left traces of what He was going to do throughout the Bible. From the beginning until His birth, it was foretold (Matthew 1:18-25). Through turmoil and tragedy, God showed Himself strong and used many people (including a prostitute named Rahab — see Matthew 1:5) for the line of King David to come through. Kingdoms were built and destroyed. People endured slavery, murder and so much more throughout biblical history.

After thousands and thousands of years, Christ was born just as it was foretold. He was God and human and His parents had to flee from those who wanted Him dead. He grew up and at the age of twelve showed others He wasn't like other children. Then, for eighteen years, we don't have any recorded history that we can find. During that time, Jesus grew up in the ghetto. Nazareth was a gutter city. His earthly father Joseph disappeared along the way all the while His earthly mother Mary was still with Him.

Jesus preached to thousands, performed miracles, and was hated for it by the religious leaders of that day. Jesus knew what He was going to face and went to pray. Here was God in the flesh, praying. His flesh wanted to run, but His Spirit wouldn't let Him. He was falsely accused, arrested, humiliated, and tortured to fulfill His destiny. Whipped mercilessly, stripped naked and paraded around by unbelievers and mocked. They spit on Him, and He was chosen to die over a known criminal who was released.

This is the same Jesus who fed thousands, rose people from the dead, cast out a legion of demons, turned water into wine, and walked on water. Power was in His Hands, and He knew it. Yet, He stayed quiet and said NOTHING. Jesus knew what was at stake. Our eternal fates were in His Hands, and He delivered. He endured the worst form of execution that humans have ever devised.

Crucifixion was not just execution, but it was a statement of Roman power. Men and women would be murdered this way while they were stripped naked and placed on the Cross with ropes or nails. Crucifixion is more than just the nails and being held high. Crucifixion was also a slow suffocation. To breathe properly, the victim had to continually move upwards and downwards on the cross because it is hard to breathe when your arms are stretched wide, and the weight of your body pulls at the shoulders. People would lose control of their bodily functions and would urinate and defecate at the bottom of the cross. It was a struggle and embarrassing. Calvary was a nasty place where blood, urine, and feces would permeate the air, along with the smell of death.

Crucifixion developed over the years. The executioners were experts at Calvary. Many times, to increase the suffering of men they would nail their "manhood" to the cross as well. With women, they crucified them face down because no one wanted to see a woman in such agony. It is said that the faces of the crucified were painful to watch. The Romans would not just murder people, but they would leave the bodies hung out there on display. It was said that some of the Caesars would show their dominance of conquest and would line the roads to any city with thousands of crucified people as a reminder that Caesar wasn't someone to be messed with[5]. I can imagine that the Pharisees and the Sanhedrin wanted to by proxy show the Jews that they had power too. Follow these teachings of this heretic and you will die just like He did. Of course, their little plan seriously backfired as the Cross is now one of the most powerful symbols of Christ's Love!

Jesus endured this torture for us. He knew everybody that would need this sacrifice. God could have hit the reset button and wiped us out. God could have condemned us to death with no mercy, but He showed us what reconciliation is up close and personal. Jesus paid it all for us and never complained and never fought back. Yet all we do is complain and fight back at Him when he gave to us freely. Jesus gave us eternal life and all we have to do is accept His salvation and repent of our sins. We didn't have our own cross even though we deserve one. We don't have to be embarrassed and stripped naked before others to pay for our sin. Jesus did that for us.

---

[5] *Appian, Civil Wars*, 1.120

So as you enter your prayer corner today, let's remember the Cross. The emblem of suffering and shame was the greatest battlefield in history. The greatest gift that saved us from Hell and damnation. He did it all for us because He first loved us. Bless God today for that love. Thank God that you answered His call to salvation. Let it resonate in you that if God didn't do all of this life wouldn't be worth living. Jesus gave us hope to be with Him one day. He did it all for us. Because He loved us in our mess and our continual rebellion against Him. To forgive and pay a bill before we ran it up is extraordinary. Who would do such things for people like us? God did.

Day 6: How Can I Love You God?

And thou shalt love the Lord thy God with all thy heart,
and with all thy soul, and with all thy mind, and with all
thy strength: this is the first commandment. — Mark
12:30 KJV

Welcome to Day 6! Today's devotional is one of the hardest and easiest things to do in our walk with God. We are in a relationship with Someone who we can't see, but we can feel and see evidence of His Love. We know how much God loves us and now we have to figure out how to love God back. God has everything and is everything, so how in the world can we love God? We are such a hot mess compared to our God and He loves us completely even though He knows exactly who we are. What can we give in such a one-sided relationship?

The answer is in today's verse. We only have ourselves, even if we don't own ourselves. Look at how we are with our little children. Our kids don't work for serious money, and they don't pay a single bill that supports their lives. Every stitch of clothing on their bodies, every meal they eat, and their shelter is provided by their parents. When babies are born, they can't feed themselves or take care of their basic needs. We have to bathe them, change their diapers when they make a mess, tend to them when they are sick, and keep dangerous things out of their mouths. It's a job we do willingly and lovingly because we love them.

Even though they technically have nothing of their own, what they DO HAVE is love for us. When that little one draws that picture of their house and family with uneven bugged-out eyes, mismatched feet and hands with a giant crooked sun with huge eyes in the sky covered with scribbles we all know deep down in our minds that it isn't the finest artwork in the world. However, when you see the words "I love you Daddy" or "I love you Mommy" scrawled over the page and it may even be misspelled, but you see the look on their faces, and it melts your heart. At that very moment, no Rembrandt or Monet in the world is more beautiful or worthy of being displayed than that drawing of crayon. Why? Because that little child gave from their heart, and it melted yours.

That's how it is with God. When we give the gift of ourselves freely and openly, it moves God's Heart. It shows Him that we love Him. We can't give God anything of value to pay for that last breath. We can't tithe our way of showing appreciation for our jobs and homes. What can we offer God in an equal exchange? We can't beat God's giving no matter how we try. We can't. We never will. We can't ever cover the price Jesus paid on the Cross. We have no way to pay for a breath on our own without help. We are outgunned, outmatched and we alone are not enough. We are like little children to God, and He knows it.

Still, we need to love God with our whole being. How do we do this you may ask? We need to give Him all of our hearts and our minds. In everything we do and in how we act. Wherever we go and how we go back and forth. We show that love with every step and breath we can. We give God praise and we fall to our faces in worship. We bow our knees in prayer and we dig deep into His Word. We give our time, our talent, and our tithe. We give all we can to God because even though it's never enough God looks at our hearts and sees our sacrifice and our gift. Like that little child with that drawing of happiness and joy to show us love, we should give our offerings to God.

So, as you enter your prayer corner today, come to God like a little child. Know that God sees your imperfections and your faults. God realizes we will come up short. God's love and gifts can never be matched. Pour your love out on Him, anyway. Realize that God still loves you despite yourself. Go to God wide-eyed and joyful while being in awe of His majesty and power. Go unafraid of our mighty God because He still knows your name and wants you to get to know Him deeply. He desires your love and relationship. He wants you to share yourself willingly with Him. Be unashamed and be open. He's waiting for you.

Day 7: No Ordinary Love

Nay, in all these things we are more than conquerors
through him that loved us. For I am persuaded, that
neither death, nor life, nor angels, nor principalities, nor
powers, nor things present, nor things to come, nor height,
nor depth, nor any other creature, shall be able to separate
us from the love of God, which is in Christ Jesus our
Lord. — Romans 8:37-39 KJV

Welcome to Day 7! We have looked at how powerful the love of God is and how deep His Love is, but today's verse is reassurance and comfort that God's Love is eternal and won't change. This is the bedrock of our faith in Christ. This isn't some ordinary statement or creed that can be overlooked or dismissed. This scripture speaks powerful words that we need to take a long look at. The Apostle Paul wrote his letter to the Romans to speak to the Christians that were living there to address their concerns and their issues like he did with the churches at Corinth, Philippi, and Colossae, and each letter was designed for the people and situations going on there. Rome was the capital of the very secular Roman Empire and the core of its pantheistic religion that centered on the gods of Olympus such as Jupiter, Juno, and Pluto. I'm sure that most of us learned about their stories and tales in school, so I won't go into details of their faith.

These "gods" were ruthless, many times immoral, deviously wicked, plotted against each other, and used human beings as pawns in their little games. These petty deities were famous for loving humanity in one minute and then punishing them the next. The Romans lived in fear of their gods and didn't want to offend any of them. They knew from their faith that the love and devotion of their gods to them were conditional to their whims and what humans did for them. It was a chaotic faith and looking at it from a Christian perspective it was stressful!

The Roman gods were the personification of how humans were in real life, except their gods had power over the elements or specific activities. Humans, just like their gods, were flawed and temperamental. Early converts to Christianity that lived in areas where Roman culture was predominant were truly caught between two worlds. They had heard the words of Paul or those who worked with him and were convinced that Jesus was The Way and followed Him for life. Paul had to reassure people that our God was not like the ones they were used to. The Roman gods would never die for them as Christ did for us. The Roman gods didn't care for them or loved them as Christ did. Sometimes we all need that reminder that what we knew before

Christ is why we left it to begin with.

Paul went into detail about the power of God's Love. He wrote that NOTHING can separate us from His Love (Romans 8:31-39). Nothing. It was absolute and would never waver. There is nothing we could do to ever change what God feels for us. Even if we don't do what we are supposed to do and live for Christ God won't stop loving us. Even if we go astray, God won't stop adoring us. Even if we turn our backs on God, God won't turn His back on us.

Paul wrote this out of his convictions, looking at his own life. Paul chased down and murdered Christians on behalf of the Jewish religious leaders of his day. Paul was a ruthless assassin, and he thought he was doing the right thing. Then Paul met Jesus for himself, and his life changed. Paul went from killing Christians to preaching the gospel himself and I'm sure people were confused or thought he was laying a trap. Paul also paid for his sins by being shipwrecked, beaten, left for dead, and going from place to place, living off of the charity of others along the way (II Corinthians 11:16-33). Paul had a hard life. His ministry was full of tragedy and during that time he witnessed the Love of God on a personal level. He saw God protect him, take care of him, and speak to him repeatedly.

Despite what Paul had done, God didn't stop loving him. Despite what we are or what we have done (or doing) God has been proven many times over that nothing will break our bond with Him. Nothing. We can screw up royally, and God will never stop loving us. Like a good Father, God loves His children like we would love our own. The scripture for today spoke to the hearts of those who were used to gods turning on them. Not our God. Our God has gone above and beyond to prove His love for us, and we should live to prove our love for Him. God has made us conquerors in Christ because God's Love isn't just a relationship, but a promise. Every obstacle and situation we endure is laced with His Love. No matter what happens God will never fail us. Never leave or forsake us. What did we deserve to have this love? Nothing.

So as you enter your prayer corner today, remember God's miraculous Love. Let it overwhelm you and split your heart wide open. Look at Paul's testimony and others who have come before us who lived lives full of trouble and pain and experienced a love like none other. Remember how God loved you despite yourself. Remember how God forgave you when you should have paid the highest price. Look back at all the times God rescued you when you should have been left to die. Remember when you rebelled against His Will and God didn't let what you deserved to come to you. His Love makes no sense and that's something to celebrate and worship Him forever!

Part III: God, Show Me Who I Am

Day 8: *God, Let Me See Me As You See Me*

*For I say, through the grace given unto me, to every man
that is among you, not to think of himself more highly
than he ought to think; but to think soberly, according as
God hath dealt to every man the measure of faith. —
Romans 12:3 KJV*

Welcome to Day 8! Eight is the number of new beginnings and I pray that after seven days of these daily devotions that your heart has been blown away by the powerful and amazing Love of Jesus. This supernatural Love makes no sense and that's okay. We don't need to understand it, but we just are compelled to embrace His Love and devote our lives to Jesus because He is everything to us and it's beautiful! There is a side effect of God's Love. It's a good one, but it is revealing and sometimes painful in a way. Let's be clear, it's not God that is hurting us here, but it is our conscience. The more God reveals Himself to us and His powerful Love it shows us some things about ourselves. God is perfect. God never lies and God never fails. God doesn't have a hidden agenda like we sometimes do. God does for us even when we do nothing for Him. Let's face the facts here… We can't measure up. We don't even come close. When we see how good God is and how much He loves us, we see ourselves for who we are. Flawed, weak, sinful, and inadequate. I know that feeling and I'm sure many of you know how that feels, too. Here is a perfect God in love with an imperfect creation and I'm sorry, but how can we not want to see ourselves?

This is where it gets interesting. We not only need to see ourselves, but we also need to see how God sees us through His eyes. Asking God to show us what we look like is a painful experience because God doesn't mince words and He doesn't leave out any details. It is a literal "come to Jesus" moment where his clarity is overwhelming, but completely necessary. We see ourselves more and more clearly as we develop our relationship with Christ. This makes us feel inadequate and the Enemy tries to slip in and use our feelings against us. He wants us to stop pushing forward because if we stay on the surface level of our walk with Christ we won't have power in Jesus and we won't be a threat to Hell. Satan knows that the Love of God is unbreakable and if he can keep us wallowing in feeling inadequate and afraid to go deeper in Jesus, he can keep us weak and afraid.

My wife loves Hallmark® movies during the Christmas season. I've watched many of them with her and believe it or not, I enjoy seeing such stories. Many of them detail how two unlikely people meet and slowly fall in love with each other before the movie is over. Many times, one of the two people sees how wonderful the other person is and sees the things they do to show love and they feel inadequate and aren't sure that they are good enough to be loved. Many times they leave or run away, and the other person chases them down, professes their love, and behold, we have a happy ending.

When we look at how wonderful God is and how deep His Love is for us, we can't help but feel inadequate. Not just one of us, but all of us. We can't measure up to God. We can't think we are any better than any other person. We aren't. We all are terrible investments. We don't cut it. We just don't. Despite that, it makes no sense at all that God has chased after us with reckless Love. It overwhelms and it is mind-boggling. Just like a parent and their baby, God has seen us at our worst. We've seen our children covered in filth and we have had to bathe them and clean them up. We have cared for them when they ate something we told them not to eat that made them sick. We have had to clean up their messes as they learn more about themselves and the world around them. We still love them no matter what don't we? God already knows us in the most intimate ways and is waiting on us to open up ourselves to Him.

God has chased us down because He loves us and, yes, we are the weaker partner in this relationship. Yes, we are full of flaws and despicable things. No, we don't deserve His Love, and yet He loves us, anyway. Instead of being down on ourselves we should lift our faces upward and let God love us. Let Him heal us and let Him build our faith in Him. Why? Because God knows who we are and still He loves us. This should cause us to continually examine ourselves and see where we need to be a better child of God. This keeps us humble and always in the pursuit of growing in Christ.

So, as you enter your prayer corner today, ask God to reveal to you how He sees you. Realize that you will feel embarrassed and inadequate, but God doesn't want you to stay in those feelings. Know that God is for us, and no one can be against us. Embrace His Love and no longer be ashamed. He is still waiting for us to plunge in, so do just that. Plunge into Jesus and know that despite yourself God won't reject you. Turn the feelings of inadequacy into even more love for Jesus. God has shown that you are worth it, so tell God that this journey is worth it. Ask Him to help you perfect yourselves in Him. God won't turn away from you.

Day 9: I Want To See Clearly

For now, we see through a glass, darkly; but then face to
face: now I know in part; but then shall I know even as
also I am known. — I Corinthians 13:12 KJV

Welcome to Day 9! This has been an amazing journey together. As I write these devotionals, I have been taking this trip along with all of you. All of us have been looking deeper and deeper inside of ourselves and at our relationship with Christ. As we look inside of ourselves, we also need to see things the way God sees things in our everyday lives. What this means is that we need not just physical eyesight, but we also need spiritual eyesight too.

Let's just make it plain and simple. God is a spirit (John 4:24). We are a spirit wrapped in a physical body, and that body limits our connection to the world. It doesn't matter if we have perfect 20/20 vision, can hear with less than twenty-five Hertz on the hearing scale, possess a trained palette that can discern every ingredient you can taste or a perception in your touch that can feel the movement of every atom. Even if we had superhuman senses and could notice a mosquito flying from miles away, we would still be inadequate. We might have the physical world covered, but what about the spiritual realm?

Without spiritual perception, we are ill-equipped for this life. Yes, God is a Spirit, but we must remember that Satan is a spiritual being, too. Demons are spirits and our enemies use spiritual tools that manifest in the physical world. When we enter a relationship with Jesus, we have crossed a picket line of sorts. When we are born into this world, we are born in sin. We are born into a realm controlled by the Adversary because of the fall of Adam. Accepting Jesus Christ as your Lord and Savior is a declaration of war against Satan. We all know that Satan doesn't handle rejection very well, so he then unleashes everything he can in the spirit realm to stop you.

Christ doesn't leave us unprepared for this fight (Ephesians 6:11-18), but we have to trust in Him and allow Him to sharpen our spiritual senses. God stands ready and protects us from dangers seen and unseen (Psalms 91:3-7). He knows what's coming our way, but the tricky part of this is us. Why? Because we have free will to choose what we want. God respects us as individuals and won't ever force Himself on us. We were created to willingly love God as conscious individuals. God will allow us to go through situations and scenarios where our spiritual senses can be sharpened.

Let's look at movies for a second. We all love those movies where someone or some creature has senses that the regular unsuspecting humans don't have. Alien hunters that can see in the dark or soldiers that have laser targeting weapons that can wipe out people without mercy. You see their fear as they know something is coming, but they don't know where it's coming from. They flail in the dark and are caught unaware until they meet their fates. It's not until the victims learn what tools and abilities their enemies have that they can defeat them and have a happy ending after being victorious.

We see through a "glass darkly" (I Corinthians 13:12) and we have to depend on God to help us see clearly. We need to have discernment of the things moving around us that have their sights set on our destruction. We also need to see God's warring angels or His Hand moving around us too (Psalms 91:11-12). Spiritual sight is required as we deepen our relationship with Jesus (II Corinthians 5:7). That's why we have the Holy Spirit to help and educate us (John 14:26). Without that spiritual connection, we are handicapped, and it's like us taking a plastic spoon to a gunfight. Without seeing the spiritual realm, we will lose. There is no other way to say this (Ephesians 6:12).

Here is some assurance. Wherever we are in Christ, we will have sight and weapons we need for that level. Jesus will not let us get torn apart by demonic wolves if we don't desire to go deeper in Him. Jesus knows the consequences of being in a relationship with Him. Christ knew what His Apostles would go through when He chose them. He knows it all and He desires the best for us. In these thirty days, we are plunging into Jesus and because of that; we need better spiritual senses. We need stronger weapons of prayer and worship. We need more study of His Word. All we have to do is ask.

So, as you enter your prayer corner admit to God that you need to see clearly. That you desire more sight and insight into the spirit realm. Pray that God opens your spiritual eyes to what hasn't been seen before. Ask God to strengthen your faith because what you will see will terrify your flesh. What you will discern will make the hairs stand up on the back of your neck. Request from the Lord that He gives you His peace as you ask God for more of Him. Just remember this one thing. What is seen can never be unseen.

Day 10: Take Me Deeper

If we say that we have fellowship with him, and walk in darkness, we lie, and do not the truth: But if we walk in the light, as he is in the light, we have fellowship one with another, and the blood of Jesus Christ his Son cleanseth us from all sin. If we say that we have no sin, we deceive ourselves, and the truth is not in us. If we confess our sins, he is faithful and just to forgive us our sins, and to cleanse us from all unrighteousness. — I John 1:6-9 KJV

Welcome to Day 10! Coming to grips with ourselves and our relationship with Jesus is truly the beginning of wisdom. Understanding that we have a responsibility to examine ourselves and realize what and who we are to God and while we should never be ashamed of ourselves in God's Presence and that we must take action and make the corrections necessary for us to be the people of God that He wants us to be. We have to go beyond knowing that God understands us, but we have to become more like Him as we humanly can. We have to know where we stand in Christ Jesus and our relationship with Him. To understand what that means is that we have to know our weaknesses and our faults and be aware of them because, as we ask God to show us who we are they will be made known to our hearts and minds. Think of it as a sort of "stress test" of where we stand.

Our world is built on safety standards and measures. Mechanical and engineering people know of the little numbers that you see on the heads of bolts as indicators of how much strain they can take by twisting or torque. Our cellphones have an Ingress Protection or IP rating of how much water they can be in before they fail. The breakers in our homes have ratings for how much electrical power in amperes or amps they can take before they trip, and the lights go out. Our scientific and mathematical models can forecast and determine how much weight and flexing a bridge can hold, how thick of a wire we need to use to plug in our favorite appliances, and how many pounds of air pressure we can put in our tires. How did these limits get set? How did we discover what was safe and effective for every aspect of our lives? Here is the simple answer. These things failed during a test.

When people swam in the rivers and oceans, they learned some very real lessons of what they could and couldn't do. We knew we needed air to survive underwater because we witnessed someone drown. So one day someone had the idea of putting a tube in their mouth that stuck out of the water. That worked until someone thought that if they went deeper, they could use a longer tube to go further into the murky depths. Well, they kept trying to push the limits with longer and longer tubes and someone eventually died because the water around their bodies crushed their chest cavities and collapsed their lungs and they suffocated and immediately drowned.

Then we got clever and realized that if we surround ourselves with wood or metal that couldn't be so easily crushed that we could breathe air in a submersible boat. That worked too for a while until they tried to go deeper and realized that the water would crush that vessel too. Someone then got the idea that they not only had to protect the vessel from being crushed, but they had to pressurize it with air to help the steel. Formulas determined the "crush depth" of a submarine or submersible vehicle after many tests in relation to the depth of the water. The only way a vehicle can be certified is for it to be checked carefully and reviewed from the inside out. Even then, as time progresses, new standards are enacted to improve safety features and, if kept up to date, they can remain in service for a long time.

To the submarine builder, it can be a humbling experience that the design they worked so hard on may or may not be up to the job it must do without a plan in place first. However, by following strict guidelines previously set by the experts a submarine can not only be certified for a certain depth but could be constructed with extra protections in case of an emergency. By getting inspections regularly and removing faulty or cheap materials and being honest with the construction, a shipbuilder can be successful and trustworthy in their craft. Any fool that doesn't follow the rules will never be considered reliable because their vessels fail every single time. Putting a weaker bolt in an engine will cause failure. Designing a bridge with weakness will cause death. Using poor quality steel can cause your ship to sink and they might make a very long three-hour movie about it one day, something like hitting an iceberg or something like that.

Our spiritual lives are the same. The scriptures have laid out the plans for our lives and the more we get to know the architect, the better equipped we can become. We free our spirits of faulty materials by confessing our sins and asking God to purify our lives (Psalms 24:3-4). Too often, we want to build our lives our way. We want the easy way in or out of situations. We want to live how we want and still serve God. Sorry, but I have news for you. It doesn't work that way. Where we were last year in Christ may not be enough for this year's devil. How we ignored that sin last month could kill us today. We should be continually revamping, renewing and improving our spiritual resistance and strengths because our Adversary isn't sitting still and will not keep using what he attacked you with last time. You won't know until you go deeper.

So, as you enter your prayer corner today, ask God to take you deeper. Take you deeper than you have ever been to see where your spiritual crush depth is. Let God show you where your weak points are. Let Him reveal where your leaks and inferior materials are located. Ask God where the problems are and confess them to Him and let God show you how to fortify and redesign your life. We all need to do it. God will not just clean you up, but He will fix you up. If you trust Him, He will never let you be crushed, but He will strengthen you and be that extra layer of protection so that you can be where you need to be. You won't know until you release your ballasts of doubt and go deeper into Him. The world of sin may try to crush you, but the Word and Spirit of God will pressurize you and the steel of faith will sustain you. You won't know how strong you are until you go deeper into the depths of our Almighty God!

Day 11: I Want More of You

*According as his divine power hath given unto us all
things that pertain unto life and godliness, through the
knowledge of him that hath called us to glory and
virtue: Whereby are given unto us exceeding great and
precious promises: that by these ye might be partakers of
the divine nature, having escaped the corruption that is in
the world through lust. And beside this, giving all
diligence, add to your faith virtue; and to virtue
knowledge; and to knowledge temperance; and to
temperance patience; and to patience godliness; and to
godliness brotherly kindness; and to brotherly kindness
charity. For if these things be in you, and abound, they
make you that ye shall neither be barren nor unfruitful in
the knowledge of our Lord Jesus Christ. But he that
lacketh these things is blind, and cannot see afar off, and
hath forgotten that he was purged from his old sins. —
II Peter 1:3-9 KJV*

Welcome to Day 11! Today's devotional will focus on how big our God is (and subsequently, how small we really are). God is so amazing! He has given so much of Himself and made such a way for us. It is overwhelming and comforting at the same time. Once we see ourselves as God sees us, it changes our perspective of how we should live. If we are willing, we will see just how massive and how small and helpless we really are. God is perfect for us and is patient with us and we should always desire to be the best we can be for ourselves and, most of all, for Christ.

I am an amateur astronomer and I love looking up at the stars and seeing the constellations and the beautiful heavenly bodies that are visible in the night sky. It doesn't matter if they are stars, planets, meteors, constellations or comets, I am in awe of the Universe on display. In the winter where the nights are longer one of the brightest stars in the sky, Sirius is a part of the constellation Canis Major or commonly known as the Big Dog. If you want to find it, look to the "southwest" of the constellation Orion in the fall and winter months and you will see it. It has been viewed for thousands of years and while it's not important for navigation, it is brilliant and has been remarked for being accurate when it shows up on the scene.

In ancient times, its arrival in the sky preceded the annual flooding of the

Nile in Egypt. It was recorded by many cultures all over the world for many reasons and causes certain familiar terms like the "dog days" of summer to be in our culture. However, in 1844, it was discovered that Sirius wasn't a single star, but had a tiny companion star that orbited around it. Sirius is known as a binary star system. A binary system has a more dominant star that causes another star to go around it like a planet does. The unique thing is that the smaller companion isn't as bright as the bigger star and not as powerful, but the smaller star follows the bigger one wherever it goes. You can't see the little star because the light of the bigger one overshadows them both. They are tied together while independent and the smaller one benefits from being protected by the bigger star. What is interesting is that the smaller star doesn't have an internal heat source of its own. It is actually a white dwarf, and it is slowly cooling and losing its brightness. It wasn't until people saw the bigger and brighter star that the little dwarf star was discovered[6]. This relationship seems quite unfair, but as stars go, it is how most of the Universe works. I know our relationship with God is much more dynamic, but it's hard not to see how we are a lot like the little star.

When we are open to God, He rubs off on us. Just like any long-term relationship, we begin to resemble the ones we are living life with. When we are in the orbit of God's glory and His Love we take on His attributes. When there is true love, we learn things about the other person, and we learn to see the things that aren't compatible with the relationship. When this happens, we don't see two, but we see one. Unified in many ways while being individuals. When people see us, they should see the glory of God foremost. We still can shine brightly, but God is still greater. We should see where we aren't like God and desire to be more and more like God, because we shouldn't want to be seen without God. We shouldn't want anything less, but to remove anything in us that would be incompatible with God.

So as you enter your prayer corner, continue to ask God to reveal to you who you are to Him. Ask God to identify those things that aren't like His. Don't be afraid of asking these questions. Desire to just orbit God and let His Glory be greater than yours. Let His power overshadow you and give you your light. Even though we are powerless compared to God, let Him empower us with His power. Let His Glory reflect off of you so that others might see God in you. Pray that God gives you the humility to allow yourself to be overshadowed by our awesome God. Pray that from afar that others see God first and you second. It's okay to be the lesser in the presence of our mighty God!

---

[6] *Sirius (Alpha Canis Majoris): Star Facts.* (2021). Sirius. https://www.star-facts.com/sirius/

Day 12: Turn On The Lights

This then is the message which we have heard of him, and declare unto you, that God is light, and in him is no darkness at all. If we say that we have fellowship with him, and walk in darkness, we lie, and do not the truth: But if we walk in the light, as he is in the light, we have fellowship one with another, and the blood of Jesus Christ his Son cleanseth us from all sin. If we say that we have no sin, we deceive ourselves, and the truth is not in us. — I John 1:5-8 KJV

Welcome to Day 12! Today's devotional will make you uncomfortable because it made me stop and think about this verse and what it means to us all. The Word of God cuts like a two-edged sword and contrary to what many churches teach that sword isn't just for the sinner, but also the saved. A lot of times, people in our local churches get too comfortable with their status when it comes to sin, and it needs to stop. We can't allow ourselves to get high and mighty with our "level" because many others are watching us. Too many hearts have gone cold because of complacency and as the Body of Christ we need to allow the whispers of God to be heard once again. The conviction of the heart of humanity was always meant for all of us to experience, and the Word of God has amplified this many, many times.

The Light of God brings healing, peace, and power, and it also brings revelation. God is a God of truth and is without sin. We have to be very careful when we desire to "walk in the light" because we could very well be uncovered and shown for what we are. That seems harsh, but we all have indeed sinned and fallen short of God's glory. If we believe we are flawless before God and we may point out everyone else's sin we truly are mistaken. Still, God is just and fair and realizes that we have to learn more of His ways so that we can be more like God in our journey. So you may ask yourself, *"What do I do?"* How in the world can we truly be in a relationship with such a powerful and Holy God? Don't worry my friends, because just like many things in this world it takes time. Sometimes more time for some than others, but our God is patient and loving.

Let me share something about myself. I am an occasional migraine sufferer. One of my triggers that causes my headaches to get out of control is bright light. When a migraine is approaching, my eyes get sensitive and to recover I need to go into a dark room and shut the door and cover the windows. Sometimes I have to stay in the dark all day, but when the pain is gone, I have to slowly turn up the lights until it gets back to normal. If I didn't? It could trigger another migraine. However, the longer I stay in the darkness the longer it takes for me to return to the light. If I never left the dark, my eyes would learn to adjust to the darkness permanently.

I had to learn how to turn up the lights in that room to return to the daytime. In our lives, sin can be like that. The pain of being separated from God's will cause us to be too sensitive to His Light and we avoid that pain and retreat into darkness. It's comfortable there and we can hide (or so we think). If we stay in sin too long, the Light of God will cause us discomfort because the Light shows us our darkness. It reveals the things we can't or don't want to see that the dark keeps from us. It hurts and if we don't lose faith and take it slow walking and growing with Christ and move more and more into His Light, we will finally be free from the darkness of sin.

Let me pause here for a moment and let you know that what I'm talking about here is the PRACTICING of sin versus the OCCASIONAL sin. We are all humans doing our best to please God and because of that, we will make mistakes and stray away from the true path of God. When we discover our error, we feel remorse and we repent to God and seek His help in restoring us back to what is right. When we choose to sin, and we don't care about the consequences, and we take advantage of God's Grace is when we truly can plunge into darkness. The Holy Spirit will nudge us and show us we are going astray and when we hear the warnings and still blatantly choose to do what we want to do because we know God won't kick us out of Heaven and that after our fun we can go back to God and repent? That is where our delusions will cause our downfall.

As Christians, we don't always know when we are moving towards darkness and sometimes, in shame, we run back to it after giving it up. God wants us to realize that we all sin and fall short (Romans 3:23). We can't fool ourselves. God sees us and He knows our struggles and as long as we realize we are flawed, weak, and prone to sin the better we are. Waking up to the reality that we need God desperately to be in fellowship with Him is a giant leap into understanding God's amazing love and patience. Believe me, this is difficult to hold on to because our Adversary wants us to wallow in shame and stay in the mediocre. We are going to mess up sometimes and try to stay where we don't have to face God. It's just important that we remember He is always just and faithful to forgive us (I John 1:9).

So, as you enter your prayer corner today, ask God to turn on His Light and search your soul. Ask Him to search your heart and mind. Ask Him to put the mirror in front of you and let you get a good, long look. Even if it hurts, let Him show you. You are safe in His Presence. Know that He already knows and loves you. Open your eyes and believe what God shows you. You are important to God. He wants your relationship, and He wants to take you places you've never been. Let His Light cleanse you and give you peace.

Day 13: Measure Me

For all have sinned, and come short of the glory of God;
— Romans 3:23 KJV

Welcome to Day 13! While today's verse has been used so often in witnessing to others that they need to be saved, God has, over my walk with Christ has shown me that it goes much deeper than that. This verse applies to the saved too and it's high time we stay vigilant in that process that keeps us humble and keeps us open to the Voice of God. Over the past few days, we've asked God to show us what we look like to Him and that we need to see clearly, but one component of seeing yourself as God sees you is realizing where you measure up AND where God wants us to be. God left us His Word to allow us to see where we are and how far on or off target we are. With His Word and His Will as our guides, we can look at ourselves and then ask God to show us whatever we are missing. That's a handful to consider, so let's dig in.

If anyone has ever been a participant in a wedding no matter if you are wearing a tuxedo or a dress, one of the tedious parts of the process is the fitting. We have to go get ourselves measured by someone because it is impossible to do it ourselves and get an accurate reading. We have to get the measurements recorded and take them to the place where we are getting the garments ordered for the big day. We have to go to wherever they measure you and we have to stand a certain way for them to measure us from head to toe. The measurements are not arbitrary. There are certain things that have to be accounted for such as inseam, outseam, and neck size. They take the information and record it on a little card and then you have to have the numbers sent away and after a bit of time the outfit is prepared, and we then get a call to set up an appointment for the dreaded fitting.

Personally, this is the part that I hate the most. During the fitting, we go into the dressing room, take our outer garments off and we try on that tuxedo or dress. We then have to step out and go before the multiple mirrors on a platform that surround us, and our measurements are verified by the person in charge of the fitting and if something needs adjustment because of our current fit for the style of the garment they are made by the seamstress or tailor and the garment is sent away again or done on the spot to be made ready and makes us look our best. The lights are bright, and you have to not only look at yourself but be looked at by others. It can feel humbling or even embarrassing, but it's necessary to be ready for the event the outfit is being prepared for.

First, let's make the most obvious statement. Measurements are taken by a universal standard. Whether it be in inches or centimeters, the ruler applied is consistent, like the Word of God is consistent and true. We can trust its measurements and its standards because they are the breathed-out words from the Creator Himself. Spiritually, we all fall short of the designs that God has set for us. We are all saved by His grace (Ephesians 2:8). We are all flawed individuals, and we can't measure ourselves and get an accurate reading. Only God can do that, and He is the best at it. Just like that custom outfit, God tailor makes our garments of holiness just for us. When we walk with God, we have to not only let Him examine us, but we need to see what He's doing. We have to stand in front of His mirrors and try on the garments of relationship that He is making for us. He desires us to be prepared and equipped in our lives with Christ. This garment we wear is preparing us for the Marriage Feast of the Lamb. We are the Bride of Christ, and we should desire to be the best we can be.

We can't always look our best for certain occasions with off-the-shelf clothes. Religion is a garment created by people based on the needs and requirements of the few and is used to apply to the many. Nothing beats a tailored outfit that is made for us and while God will see us as acceptable as just being saved why not let Him measure us for a custom relationship with Him He can cover our bulges and accentuate our best features not just to God, but to others? We can't just put on religion and be all that God wants us to be because it is a human construct. Every relationship is unique. What works for one person won't work for another. Jesus knows that we all fall short of His glory, and He wants to show us the measurements so that we can see what we need to be the best we can be for Him.

Knowing where we measure up allows us to figure out how far we have to go to get in line with the Word of God, too. Yes, God can cover our mistakes and build things around us, but we should also want to do our part and put in the work to fit what God has made just for us. Just like that tuxedo or dress for that occasion, sometimes we have to lose a little weight or maintain our weight so that we will still fit what the measurements say. God works with us, and we need to work with Him and be an active participant in the process of our spiritual growth.

So, as you enter your prayer corner today, ask God to measure you. Let Him show you how you measure up to Him and then let Him prepare you to be well dressed for what He desires for you. Let God mold and shape you by His design and not your own. Pray that God lets you see what He has for you. Let God revise your view of how He wants to see you. Submit to the Will of God and let Him alter you. Let Him reassure you and He will prepare and clothe you for the road ahead. His Love covers a multitude of sins, and He wants you to be ready to walk by that Devil and show him you are tailor made for Jesus!

Day 14: Stripped Down and Purified

*And he shewed me Joshua the high priest standing before
the angel of the Lord, and Satan standing at his right
hand to resist him. And the Lord said unto Satan, The
Lord rebuke thee, O Satan; even the Lord that hath chosen
Jerusalem rebuke thee: is not this a brand plucked out of
the fire? Now Joshua was clothed with filthy garments
and stood before the angel. And he answered and spake
unto those that stood before him, saying, Take away the
filthy garments from him. And unto him he said, Behold, I
have caused thine iniquity to pass from thee, and I will
clothe thee with a change of raiment. — Zechariah 3:1-4
KJV*

Welcome to Day 14! I will not cut cards with you. We are in the fight of our lives. The Adversary wants to stop us from growing in Christ and will do anything he can to either slow us down or stop us. The thing that we have to remember is that while God is working on us, the Enemy is right there, doing what he does best. He is the accuser of humanity and since he convinced or led us into sin, he tries to tattle on us. Satan knows that God already knows what we are and doing and all he's doing is taunting us and making us feel guilty.

A long time ago there was a boy who went to visit some relatives and once there they went out with the boys and their friends to go play some football. They were having a great time tossing the ball, catching passes, and scoring touchdowns, all while everyone enjoyed the summer sun. The boys were near a park-like area near some trees, and someone threw a pass that was missed, and the ball tumbled into the woods. They were all out waiting when suddenly a boy from the woods yelled out, *"Come over and see this!"* Now, as you know, young boys have little good sense and what this one kid found was a hornet's nest in the hollow of a tree.

Most of these kids were from the suburbs and this one lad was from the country, so he was familiar with some things they weren't. That boy ran up with everyone else (as silly boys do) to see what was going on and when he saw what was there, he immediately stopped dead in his tracks. He knew that this wasn't something to fool around with. He tried to let them know they were playing with fire and that they needed to leave that hornet's nest ALONE. By this time, the presence of all of those bodies had caused a few hornets to fly around the nest and his instincts were screaming for him to get out of there. Some heeded the country boy's warning while others decided they were going to see what happened next. As they got closer, he decided that he did his part to warn them, and he bolted for the quickest escape route out of there. Not even two minutes passed, and a loud blood-curdling scream rang out and every boy that stayed over there took off running except for the one unfortunate soul who was sadly the victim.

One boy (in his "infinite" wisdom) decided it was a good idea and would be a lot of fun to urinate on the hornet's nest and that didn't sit well with those now circling hornets. As this boy ceremoniously aimed his pee shooter at this nest, one hornet flew out and sting the source of the impromptu rainstorm that was destroying their house and let's just say it became a situation not easily forgotten for this young boy. To make matters worse, it turns out he was allergic to bee stings (and obviously hornets) and after being stung on the you-know-what by an angry hornet he had passed out from the venom of the sting (and probably the pain) with the now rapidly swelling stung area waving in the breeze. About ten minutes later, an ambulance pulled up because someone ran back to their house and told their Mom what had happened. We ran back towards the commotion at the scene (like boys do) to look at who it was and what happened, and it wasn't pretty. The EMTs had to grab him, run from the area and then strip him down, treat the sting, and give him a shot of epinephrine to save his life. All while the boy who found the nest (and we found out later was the one who dared the other boy to pee on it) was telling the paramedics, *"I told him not to mess with it!"* all while this now thoroughly embarrassed boy was being wheeled away to the ambulance.

Here's the beautiful part of this story. The EMTs didn't pay any attention to the boy accusing the one who was hurt. Once she treated his wound after being exposed, she covered him up with a fresh gown, held his hand, and let him know he was going to be okay. This young man's parents were at work, so no one was there for him, and this paramedic stepped up because she was probably a mother herself. After tending to the victim, she told the tattling boy to leave the hurt one alone and for him to go home. This boy had gone through enough and didn't need to be embarrassed any further. She had embodied compassion at its highest degree. God does that with us spiritually. The Devil will point his finger at us when God is cleaning us up and God will rebuke Satan while He works on you. God already knows that our righteousness is already like filthy rags (Isaiah 64:6) and He doesn't care. Because God loves us, and the price has already been paid for our sins and He wants to get you out of those filthy ways and put on some clean ones.

So as you enter your prayer corner today, remember as you are asking God to show you what you look like that the Adversary will try to whisper in your ear and tell you that you aren't good enough. Why bother? You'll be right back where you were. He'll tell you that God doesn't need a messed-up person like you. Rebuke that devil in the Name of Jesus and let God continue to clean you up and put His fresh garments on you. God doesn't care that you're dirty, He only wants you to come to Him. That's it. Come with a heart that's broken for God. Come and let God wash you clean. Know that God only wants what's best for you. It doesn't matter what it was. It doesn't matter how deep it is. Just let God take it off of you. It's okay.

Day 15: How God Made Us

*And God said, Let Us make man in our image, after our
likeness: and let them have dominion over the fish of the
sea, and over the fowl of the air, and over the cattle, and
over all the earth, and over every creeping thing that
creepeth upon the earth. So God created man in His own
image, in the image of God created he him; male and
female created He them. — Genesis 1:26-27 KJV*

Welcome to Day 15! Realizing who we are and how God sees us is a tough journey, but it is worth the trouble that it seems to bring. However, we need to go to the beginning and see where we came from. We need to understand how and why God made us how He did. Today's verse gives us insight into the day of Creation that God said was VERY good (Genesis 1:31)! I've often wondered what the verse meant when it said, *"Let Us make man in Our image, after Our likeness"* and I truly believe that God gave me a revelation into those statements. Because God said it that way, it has to have a meaning important to our existence.

First, look at the words "in Our image" and let that marinate for a little bit. What is an image? One definition could be "A representation of the form of a person or object, such as a painting or photograph."[7] When we take a picture of a person or place, we take a three-dimensional object and capture it into a two-dimensional image. Depending on the camera, the density or quality of the image is measured in megapixels. The more megapixels, the better the resolution. We can see colors, light, and shadows, but the image is one dimension less than the real thing. So I can imagine that when God in His image He made us a few dimensions less than Himself. God is everywhere, and we are in one place. God knows everything and we are limited. We are a flesh limited snapshot of God.

So what about likeness? Likeness can be defined as the state, quality, or fact of being like or resembling, a similar appearance, or sculptured representation of something. I know that's a lot of words, but let me try to explain. Likeness means that we are made the same way and have some of the same attributes. Like a statue of a person, it captures what they look like and when you see that statue it reminds you of the original. A likeness is not a direct copy. God has feelings, thoughts and free will just like we do. He can

---

[7] Image. The American Heritage dictionary of the English language. (2000). Boston: Houghton Mifflin.

change His mind just like we can. God can speak things into existence. We too have that ability, but it is limited because we need faith in God to activate it (Romans 4:17).

Psalms 139:14 says that we are fearfully and wonderfully made. Fearfully, when translated from the Hebrew means with great reverence, heart-felt interest, and with respect. Wonderfully, when translated from the Hebrew, means unique and set apart. God took the time to make us to resemble Him and to relate to Him. What other creature on Earth can do that? Yes, other things have high intelligence, can solve problems, make tools and even communicate with us through language, but what other creation besides humans can reason with and be in relationship with God? I dare say none of them can because God made us with great reverence, heart-felt interest and respect. We are set apart because we look like God. We aren't God even though the Serpent tricked Eve into thinking so because it was a half-truth (Genesis 3:5).

So the Adversary doesn't want you to know who you are because he really knows. He wants you to think that you don't have a choice in how your life will be. He wants you to think that you are powerless against demonic forces. He doesn't want you to know how special you are to God. When God looks at us, He sees a being He sculpted from the dust of the ground Himself. God Himself took the rib from Adam and made Eve. God spoke everything else into existence, but formed humanity from the dust on the ground. He shaped us and He made us different from everything else that was made. We were intentional. We were designed and we are unique. Our kinship to God is so special that He made us joint-heirs with Christ who is His only begotten Son (Romans 8:16-18). That's just an outstanding thing that our God loves us so much!

So, as you enter your prayer corner today, remember that you are a son or daughter of God. God sees you as a special creation that He loves and cares deeply about you. That's why He gave you so many chances to get it right with Him. God won't throw you away because of this unique relationship He has with you. He sees us as children because we were made to look like Him even though we can never be Him. Plunge into the arms of a God who formed us. Ignore the chattering of the Adversary and of our flesh that tells you that you will never be enough. God knows who you are, and He made you beautiful. God already can see who and what you are and still adores you. Even in your mess, He is there for you. Let Him love you. Let Him heal you. Let Him restore you. Give it all to Him and let Him show you where to begin.

Part IV: God, Prepare Me

Day 16: Fired Up & Ready To Go

Be thou prepared, and prepare for thyself, thou, and all thy company that are assembled unto thee, and be thou a guard unto them. — Ezekiel 38:7 KJV

Welcome to Day 16! This day marks the second half of this series of devotionals of thirty days of fresh fire. Our God has always been with us, and He has proven that time and time again. Throughout the scriptures, God has also stressed the importance of community. Even though we have to be prepared, we also have to prepare others around us for this journey. I know that this seems a little on the personal side, but we are members of ONE BODY in Christ Jesus (I Corinthians 12:12-27). We can't forget that the Bible calls us the Bride of Christ (II Corinthians 11:2, Ephesians 5:27, Revelation 19:7) and on a smaller note the Apostle Paul wrote letters to the churches of entire cities. Being in Christ means God is with us AND within us there are other smaller groups of people.

Just about every time God has performed a miraculous action that was seen by non-believers, there has been more than one person doing it. Noah built the Ark with his sons. Abraham received God's promise but needed Sarah to fulfill it. Gideon needed three hundred men to defeat Israel's enemies. King David had groups of elite warriors in their conquests for Israel. Jesus, even though He didn't need them, had twelve apostles. During the Early Church, missionaries were sent out from Jerusalem two by two. Paul had Silas, and I'm sure you get the idea. I'm hoping that this thirty-day journey that you are not alone and that you are bonded together with others because community is so important.

I will never forget going to the Inauguration of President Barack Obama on a frozen morning on January 20, 2009. Thousands of people came to Washington, DC and I will never forget running across the National Mall at 5 AM to get as close as I could to witness the event. It was bitterly cold that morning. We were all thronged together in unity and the sense of community that elected our 44th President spilled over to that gathering. It was freezing and we all shared personal heat aids, gave elderly people our extra scarves, hats, and gloves to whomever needed them and didn't worry about getting them back. People shared their packed sandwiches with those that had nothing to eat. While we waited and watched the sun rise over the Capitol Dome, excited people were chanting *"FIRED UP! READY TO GO!"* as we waited until the Oath of Office was given and a new President took command of our nation. I remember how people were leading others into morning devotions and scripture readings. Some people were doing jumping jacks and running in place to help each of us to keep moving and stay warm. People were singing old spirituals and hymns. We were fired up and ready. We were a total community with one goal. We were many folks, but we were one people.

As we go through this walk with Jesus, we have to reach out to our brothers and sisters and care for them as we would ourselves. We must never forget that we are meant to be joined as one people. The Enemy loves to isolate us just like a lion looks for the slowest or weakest gazelle. We may not be the strongest, but we have to help each other in whatever way we can. When we confront things in life, it is okay to reach out to someone you trust, or God has to lead you to for help. Remember, it is when two or three are gathered together in God's Name that He is with us (Matthew 18:20). With God with us, who can be against us (Romans 8:31)? These things alone should have you pumped up and ready to achieve whatever God has for your hands to do! Can God do it with just Him alone? Yes, He can, but God wants us to band together too as one and unite with power. One can chase a thousand, but two can make ten thousand runs for their lives (Deuteronomy 32:30)!

Being in one community and having one goal scares the Adversary. We, as the Body of Christ, are so fragmented and separated from each other over silly things such as the songs we sing, the way we pray, how we baptize, or what day we worship. As humans, we may choose how we serve and worship God, but we shouldn't let it divide us from the war that affects us all. If you love Jesus, know that He is God (because the Three are One) in the flesh that died for the sins of the world and rose again with all power in His hands on the third day? I can be your brother in Christ. Hell has us so focused on our differences that we are not paying attention to the spiritual war all around us. We may all be different, but if we serve the God of Israel let's put our traditions and differences to the side and unite as one and get fired up and ready to go!

So, as you enter your prayer corner today, ask God to fire you up and get you ready to go to war in the Spirit. Pray that God binds you together with like-minded, fire-breathing believers that will walk with you and be there for you and you for them. Ask God to lead you to the right person to unite with in faith. For married couples, pray that God deepens your relationship together in Christ to make that three-strand cord that is not easily broken. Pray that God builds up your families to be united under The Cross. Pray that your ministry group or church unites under the Blood-Stained banner of Jesus Christ. Believe and know that we may be at war, but never alone as we march on this Battlefield of The Lord!

Day 17: I Want To Be Ready

*Humble yourselves therefore under the mighty hand of
God, that he may exalt you in due time: Casting all your
care upon him; for he careth for you. Be sober, be vigilant;
because your adversary the devil, as a roaring lion,
walketh about, seeking whom he may devour: — I Peter
5:6-8 KJV*

Welcome to Day 17! Getting to know our God is a beautiful journey, but it also has a cost. The Adversary hates us. With his whole being, he despises us and wants us to fail. His hatred is personal towards us, and it's directed at God. He wants the images of God to fail and fall so that he can rub it in God's face as he is finally cast into Hell for the last time. Lucifer was thrown out of heaven because he started a rebellion over his own pride and took a third of the angels with him (Revelation 12:3–9). He was kicked out and even though he still presents himself before God; he does nothing but bad-mouth humanity to God (Job 1:6). Let's look at why.

Lucifer was one of the most beautiful creations ever. Some Bible scholars say that he made music as he walked. He stood over God and was the anointed cherub that covered (Ezekiel 28:14). He was an amazing being and then pride set in because he thought he should be the Most High. God threw him out and then sometime later He created us in God's image. Lucifer most likely watched when we were created, and he immediately despised us. He went to work to make humanity sin and get separated from God out of spite. He's been there to stop us, misdirect us, and try to make us a disappointment to God. He knows how to defeat us if we fall for his weapons. He has legions of help that are "dead demons walking" and he doesn't care about our consequences. He knows he will be condemned to Hell, and he wants to take as many people as he can with him.

The Bible says that the fool says in their heart that there isn't a God (Psalms 14:1). I say that the bigger fool is the one who denies that the Devil is after them. The best defense against an enemy who hates us, and hates God is drawing closer to God. Those who are saved cannot be directly defeated by Satan, but can be neutralized by keeping them at a point of zero growth and a minimal relationship with Christ. For those who work in any sort of ministry capacity, your mugshot photo is up on the wall at the central post office in Hell. You are Hell's Most Wanted, and they all want you to be destroyed. That's okay. We just need to be ready.

Being ready means being in a close relationship with God and knowing the tools you have at your disposal, but the first step is total submission to

God. It's crazy to think that in order to win that you have to surrender, but that is exactly what we have to do. We have to lay "self" down and pick up the mantle that Christ has for us. We can call the Name of Jesus all we want, we can yell as loud as we can and we can have all the anointing oil and prayer cloths we can buy, but until we submit to Christ and surrender to His will we will never defeat Satan. That is frightening and goes against what many of us were taught in church growing up or even right now as you read this. There is zero authority over Satan without submission to God.

Our hearts need to burn with the desire to submit to God and His righteousness because if we don't we could get surprised. Desire, however, isn't enough because we have to put that desire into action. We have to remember and know that God is in control. God is the supreme authority, and we can't do a single thing without Him. Without submission, we would walk into a dangerous situation with the forces of Hell. We could be trapped with no escape and blindsided by what happened. Thank God for His Holy Spirit, Who is there for us in every situation. He is there for us, and His voice guides us and gives us peace. To know His voice, you have to be in a relationship with Him. When we burn for God, He will show us the things in our own lives that make us vulnerable. Remember that a chain is as strong as it's the weakest link. The flesh is always the weakest link, and we can only tame the flesh through Jesus Christ!

So, as you enter your prayer corner today, ask God to make you ready. Ask Him to show you any places in your life that Satan can take you over. It can be small or great. Until we see the vulnerable spots, we can't defeat an enemy who's great at finding them. Without that connection to God, we won't recognize the warnings or the danger. We can't see what God sees because we haven't asked Him or let Him reveal things to us. Spiritual sight comes from being closer to the Light who is Jesus Christ. Otherwise, you'd be out there all alone as gravy covered lion food. Trust me when I tell you that the devilish lion is hungry, and he will devour you (I Peter 5:8).

Day 18: Working It Out

Nevertheless, the foundation of God standeth sure, having this seal, The Lord knoweth them that are his. And, Let every one that nameth the name of Christ depart from iniquity. But in a great house, there are not only vessels of gold and of silver, but also of wood and of earth; and some to honor, and some to dishonor. If a man therefore purge himself from these, he shall be a vessel unto honor, sanctified, and meet for the master's use, and prepared unto every good work. — II Timothy 2:19-21 KJV

Welcome to Day 18! Being a vessel that God desires to use is honorable as well as humbling. God can choose to use whomever He desires and as we continue this journey of consecration, we have to stay mindful that as workers in ministry we have to strive to stay clean and stay as free from sin as we can. Yes, we are still in flesh, but that doesn't excuse us from spiritual hygiene at all. Unless we realize we cannot (and frankly should not) try to be sanctified without God's help, we are truly fooling ourselves.

Christ has given us all the tools that we need to be spiritually prepared for whatever it is God has for us to do. Many scriptures in the Bible refer to being prepared, sanctified, and clean to serve God. Whether it be our minds, hearts, and even hands God has spoken over and over about the importance of being clean. It is strange, however, that scripture tells us we've all sinned and fallen short of God's glory and that our righteousness is like filthy rags (Isaiah 64:6). That's harsh and considering the reference it makes sense. Not to point out people who menstruate, but before the modern conveniences of menstrual pads, tampons and even medications menstrual bleeding was "contained" by stuffing old pieces of unwanted fabric to collect the emissions. During the days of the Law, a woman was considered "unclean" until after seven days of being off of her period. The rags were seen as disgusting and likely thrown into the fire and not used again. Think about just how deep that is in relation to our righteousness!

In America, most people love to go out now and then and get a meal at a restaurant, whether it be fast food or gourmet. After taking our seat at a nice place, most of us will start looking at everything around us. We gaze at the silverware and the glassware looking for spots or filth. We examine the tables, floors, and even the menus themselves. We will go to the bathrooms and immediately judge how clean it could be in the kitchen (thank you to my Late Grandma T for that tidbit of wisdom!) If we see anything dirty we want to speak with a manager about it. If the fork or glass has spots, we want a fresh one. If the bathroom is nasty, we want it cleaned. We will demand justice to be served and we want it NOW!

Being clean in places that provide service for consumption is not only hoped for, but it's (thankfully) required. Health departments have regulations and procedures put in place to make things hygienic, presentable, and most importantly safe from illnesses and diseases being spread. When I was a teenager, my first job was a restaurant as a dishwasher. I was required to use an automatic dishwasher that had chemical agents that were injected during the wash and rinse cycles. These agents included detergents, degreasers and a sanitizing agent to kill the germs. The machine also had temperature-controlled water jets that shot out over the payload that were near the boiling point. This thing would dissolve the most stuck-on foods on dishes and pots and pans that I could never imagine coming off. Even though it was amazing to see in action and dishes got clean if the chemical mix was off or if something else splattered on something after being cleaned, it was always sent back to the kitchen to be cleaned again.

The thing about the dirty items at a restaurant is that they aren't thrown away. They are just sent back to be rewashed and put back into service. It didn't matter if it were a plastic drinking glass or an ornate serving platter, if it needed cleaning, it would be sent back to be washed. Spiritually, God cleans us up all the time IF we let Him. It doesn't matter if you park cars, clean toilets, usher, sing, preach, or Pastor God will lovingly take the time to clean you up if you are filthy. He prepared us for His service and even if we are found with a spot or blemish, He won't get so disgusted with us that He will throw us in the trash. God gives us a chance to get it right with Him and get back out there to be used. Unlike dishes at a restaurant, we have a choice if we want cleaning, and we can refuse. God will never force us to submit to cleaning, but He will let His intentions be known. He loves us and He wants us, but we have to choose to go back and get cleaned up if we aren't fit to serve.

Here is the part that we also have to remember. We can't clean ourselves. We can't prepare ourselves effectively because we are in the flesh. Remember when I said if the dishwasher machine's chemical mix was off that things didn't get clean? That's what happens if we try to do this job ourselves spiritually. Our mix will be off the mark. We will think we need this and not that, and we will be unfit to be used. The soap may get the dirt off that we can see, but the sanitizer removes the germs we can't see. When we try to remove the stains of sin and error, we may look clean to the human eye, but God, with His all-seeing eye knows where the spiritual germs are. Going back into service with spiritual germs could get someone infected with a spiritual disease.

So, as you enter your prayer corner today, ask God to inspect you from the inside out. We may have gone through the processes like church and such, but we still may have spots and we may be infected by spiritual germs. We still may have some other small imperfections that we aren't aware of. Ask God to prepare you for greater things. Ask God to shine you up and make you whole. Know that God realizes your imperfections and won't throw you away unless you want Him to and trust me when I tell you that He doesn't. Trust that God wants you to work it all out and be a vessel ready for Him to use. Just trust the process!

Day 19: Equip Me For The Fight

Finally, my brethren, be strong in the Lord, and in the power of his might. Put on the whole armor of God that ye may be able to stand against the wiles of the devil. For we wrestle not against flesh and blood, but against principalities, against powers, against the rulers of the darkness of this world, against spiritual wickedness in high places. — Ephesians 6:10-12 KJV

Welcome to Day 19! I know that in this series of devotionals; I have said it many times that we are at war, and I won't ever back down on that. When we become saved, we get enlisted into God's Army and we do so by defecting from the Kingdom of Darkness. Because of the fall of Adam, we were born in sin, and we needed to be reconciled with Christ (II Corinthians 5:17-21). Those who work in ministry are on another level of targeting because we are working to reach those lost in sin by the power of God as we serve to get people saved or delivered. Hell hates us, and we have to be prepared.

I love Ephesians Chapter 6 because there is a lot in that chapter about being in the fight. The Armor of God is one of the greatest illustrations of what being equipped by God means. Using the armor of a Roman soldier as a guide Paul details how the armor is composed of the Belt of Truth, the Breastplate of Righteousness, the Gospel of Peace, the Shield of Faith, the Helmet of Salvation, and the Sword of the Spirit. We've all seen that before, but have you noticed something about this list? There is absolutely nothing that covers the back of the person. Why is that?

Let's use history as our example. Most empires and civilizations in ancient times never armored the backs of soldiers because none of their soldiers should ever have to run. In medieval times, the chest plate was always thicker in the average suit of armor. Spacecraft have always had heat resistant tiles installed on the bottom of the craft that re-enters the atmosphere and never all over it. Battleships had a thick belt of steel armor around the waterline and didn't worry as much about the upper decks of the ships as well as they protected the sides from torpedoes. More defenses are placed in the areas that have the highest or perceived threat of attack or damage.

Paul detailed the Armor of God of a person who was always going FORWARD and not running away. God has given us the means to run from the Enemy. In His Word, He also said that nothing would catch us unaware. God has equipped us and prepared us to always combat our issues or enemies HEAD-ON! Our enemies are cowards and always try to attack us from behind. Thankfully protects us on every side (Psalms 139:5-6). We don't need to be afraid of the enemies by day or the fire by night (Psalms 91:5). What a blessing!

Now here comes the part we don't like to hear. We have to maintain our armor and our defenses. The major tactic of operating in a war isn't just fighting the enemy directly. You can't win a war with just brute force or sheer numbers. The greatest preparation and strategy of war is being prepared for the fight. The items listed in the Armor of God have to be spiritually maintained by each individual. We have to keep our faith growing and strong (2 Thessalonians 3:3). We need to continually study the Word of God (II Timothy 2:15). We have to keep our feet walking in the Gospel of Peace (Ephesians 6:15). We have to clean the rust spots off of the Breastplate of Righteousness (Ezekiel 18:5-9). We have to keep our Helmet of Salvation on and properly fitted (Psalms 37:39). We have to stay ready to wield the Sword of the Spirit (Hebrews 4:12). We must keep that Belt of Truth secure in our lives so that we live honestly (Proverbs 12:17).

Most importantly, we can never run from the path God has for us. We can never surrender. Why? Because His Spirit will always guide and protect us, and we don't need spiritual armor for our backs. God is all around us! We are not designed to run from Hell, but we are equipped by our Lord Jesus Christ to run into the Enemy head-on and not be afraid. Read Ephesians Chapter 6 about the Whole Armor of God and you will find that there is boldness for the wearer and no place for fear or surrender. God made us to be winners to win and He made it so that if we let go and let God nothing is impossible!

So, as you enter your prayer corner today, ask God to fit your armor to your spirit. Ask God to strengthen you and prepare you for what you must do for Him. Pray that God reveals to you where your rust spots are and ask Him how you can get them polished. Ask God to show you more and more where there is danger and how to prepare for any coming tests. Open your hearts for instruction and your spirit for correction. Ask God to give you a "Never give up, never surrender" level of faith.

Day 20: We Are At War

For though we walk in the flesh, we do not war after the flesh: (For the weapons of our warfare are not carnal, but mighty through God to the pulling down of strong holds;) Casting down imaginations, and every high thing that exalteth itself against the knowledge of God, and bringing into captivity every thought to the obedience of Christ; —
II Corinthians 10:3-5 KJV

Welcome to Day 20! This state of being in a spiritual war is one of the toughest things for many Christians to get a clear understanding of. I know we have talked about it before, but now we need to dig deeper and truly fathom what's at stake and what we can do about it. This may be a spiritual war, but we can't ever be spectators. The moment we accepted Jesus Christ as our Lord and Savior we became a participant of the battle that has been going on since Lucifer was evicted from Heaven. Contrary to public belief, our participation in this was not optional.

Let's look at our Enemy for a moment. Even though our Adversary has already lost the war, he is highly organized and frighteningly disciplined. Demons and the forces of Hell are assigned to regions and areas, and they rule over them. How do we know? Remember when Jesus was casting out the demons named Legion that they asked Jesus for permission to stay in the region (Matthew 8:31)? Then, after leaving the man, the now possessed pigs ran off of a cliff and the pigs died. Think about that for a minute. The demons asked to not leave the region. Some regions in this world have associated spirits with them and they specialize in a specific type of sin or behavior.

Hell's forces not only have supernatural power, but they rule over earthly powers (Ephesians 6:12). Remember when Jesus was tempted (Luke 4:1-13)? Satan showed Jesus all the kingdoms of the world and said that he would give them to Christ if Jesus would simply worship him. Why? Because Jesus was God and a man in flesh! He was hoping to turn the flesh side of Jesus to his favor, but it failed. Satan has potent influence over the things of this world. Sometimes, the blessings we think came from God were actually counterfeit blessings that Satan sent first to get us off course.

From Day One Satan has been on a mission to subvert and destroy the works of God. From Adam and Eve until now, our Enemy has been hard at work and using humans to do a lot. He bragged about it to God when Job's story was told that he was roaming the earth looking for whom he could devour. When someone enters ministry, they will face a powerful foe if they don't rely solely on Jesus to be with them. Why do you say that? Ask those that tried to cast out demons and they spoke to them saying *"Jesus and Paul we know, but WHO ARE YOU?"* before beating the living daylights out of them, causing them to run away naked (Acts 19:15).

You may say, *"Didn't they command them in the Name of Jesus?"* and you would be correct. Here's the reality in all of this. You may know the Name, but do you truly know Jesus? Do you have permission to use His Name out of being in a relationship with God or do you use it out of showmanship? Are you operating for the Kingdom of Heaven or the adoration of humanity? Perhaps you are just simply untrained in how spiritual warfare really works? My guess is that most people fall into that category. So many have been duped by poor teaching on how to engage demonic forces and have confronted them and sadly lost. Some give up and never fight again and others keep plodding along, getting beaten up and living defeated lives. Let's not go down that road. Let's be smart, alert and equipped soldiers in a war for lost souls and our lives.

We can win a war and lose individual battles. God has given us the tools and the equipment to be successful and victorious in this fight. The closer we come to Jesus, the more the attacks will come. The dirty tactics will play out. The flaws we have will be exposed and exploited. We have to be ready to not just prepare, but learn on the fly with the Holy Spirit as our teacher. We can't use the name of powerful people on Earth without knowing them first. If we try, we will get called out as frauds. The same goes with Jesus because the forces of Hell know who knows God. After all, when we call on the Name of Jesus with authority stuff happens in the spirit and in the natural. When you know Jesus deeply, He will withhold nothing good from you that are called according to His purpose (Psalms 84:11). Nothing.

So, as you enter your prayer corner today, ask God to prepare you for this spiritual war. Ask God to empower your faith and to strengthen your resolve. Ask God to reveal to you how to fight those demons that oppress you. Ask God to reveal to you the attachments and openings in your spirit because of previous sin or abuse. Pray that God heals any wound that can open a crack in your armor that Satan can use. Pray that God gives you the strength to go THROUGH and OVERCOME. Surrender your will to Jesus and pledge your undying loyalty to Him because He pledged His to you.

Day 21: Avoiding Pitfalls

*Beware lest any man spoil you through philosophy and
vain deceit, after the tradition of men, after the rudiments
of the world, and not after Christ.* — Colossians 2:8 KJV

Welcome to Day 21! This journey of consecration has been quite an experience and I pray that as we prepare for whatever God has us to do for Him, we are reminded that no matter how much we prepare we have to be careful not to fall short of fall into spiritual traps meant to steal our zeal and stunt your growth. Ministry can be a great blessing or a great curse and depending on how we treat it different pathways will open up for us and one of them is the road to failure. How does that happen you may ask? Satan happens. We may not be able to be possessed by demonic forces, but we can be oppressed, fooled, and defeated by them if we aren't careful.

We all have seen many religious figures rise and fall in our lifetimes. I will not name names because I don't believe in shaming or embarrassing the ministries or legacies of those who have gone or go in the name of the Lord. What I have seen is how many start on fire for Jesus and end up falling and many times falling hard. Leaders who preached heavily against a very specific sin and end up falling to it. How some have claimed to hear the Voice of God and spoke in error or spoke from their flesh. These are the same people who have gifts and talents from God that have yielded miracles, signs, and wonders and live in secret or not-so-secret sin. It's crazy!

This is why we have to hold fast to the Word of God and the Holy Spirit to be our guides in this journey with God and especially in ministry. We can't lean on every word that comes from humans, but from every word that comes from the true mouth of God (Matthew 4:4). If we go foolishly forward, we can fall back into sin and the consequences of sin. We have to be ready to face not just the scrutiny of God, but also the scrutiny of humanity. We may be instruments of God, but even the most special and revered instrument in an orchestra can get out of tune and need adjustment.

God desires us to plunge into Him and be in a relationship with Him on a deeper level. If we aren't honest with Him (even though He already knows) about the flaws we have (sin or not) we can be led astray. We need God to unpack these things and let Him work on them. Now before you think about it, let me be clear, you don't need to confess everything to everyone. Some things are deep, dark secrets that are embarrassing, so let Jesus be your guide as to how you work these things out.

Let's be real, some of you have been raped, molested, done serious drugs, murdered people, or committed serious crimes (just to name a few examples) and most people do not know that it happened to you or that you did it. Some of us have done things that if people knew they would disown us forever. Some of us have gotten distracted because we are popular among people for what we do in ministry. We may sing like a nightingale or preach the paint off the walls, but we have gotten full of pride. We may be attached to a dead organization or dead doctrine. Whether it was done to you, done by you, or indulged in by you, it has to be corrected before the Adversary uses it to tear you apart.

We can no longer live in denial of the truth about ourselves and about the positions we hold in ministry. We represent Christ. We represent the possible only light the lost will see in this world and we have to be careful. Going around with unresolved issues is a recipe for disaster. This is a tough conversation to have with yourself and our loving God. He already knows and still gives us the chance to get it right and get back in line. We simply cannot allow ourselves to trip over ourselves in this fight. Satan loves to "keep his hands clean" when it comes to ruining us and if we fall into the trap we made because we refused to deal with the hurts, the pain and the sin it's our fault. Don't blame the devil when it was you that did it.

So, as you enter your prayer corner today, ask God to show you your pitfalls. Pray that God cancels your subscriptions to things that can work against you. Pray that God can heal the dark places that others have hurt or violated you. Ask God for repentance for anything you may have done to someone else. Fervently pray that God reveals any attachments that you may have to darkness and ask Him to set you free in the Name of Jesus. Plead the Blood of Jesus against any assignments Hell may have on you. Ask Jesus to close all doors to hidden sins, agendas, doctrines, habits, and ways. Ask the Holy Spirit to fill every vacancy left by demonic presences. Then bless God for the victory!

Part V: God, Teach Me

Day 22: The Pursuit of Wisdom

The heart of the prudent getteth knowledge; and the ear of the wise seeketh knowledge. — Proverbs 18:15 KJV

Welcome to Day 22! From the moment we are born until we die, we as humans are always learning even if we realize it or not. Our level of learning depends on how we absorb and then apply new knowledge. Because our human senses are always registering the surrounding things which shape us if we are listening (sometimes even if we're not). Our spiritual senses are not any different. Our spirits absorb things around us whether or not we see them, so it's in our best interest to allow the greatest teacher of all the Holy Spirit to keep us attentive in class.

We are at a great disadvantage when it comes to our lifetimes. We are in direct contact with an Adversary that has been present throughout (and actually BEFORE) our entire human existence. Hell has been studying humanity for thousands of years, and they know how to expertly break us. Demons know how to destroy us and how to exploit unnumbered vulnerabilities in just about every situation. Demonic generational curses have traveled so far down our family trees that we don't know where the curse started. The great accuser has so much dirt on humanity and knows what we like and what makes us move. We have no secrets that Hell isn't aware of. That's a scary thing.

Therefore, we have to run to God and ask Him to teach us about spiritual matters and life. God made everything, and that includes us. Who else is better suited to show us the way? What better source can we have to teach us than the Word of God? The scriptures detail just about everything we need to know about how to not only to combat the Devil but also how to live. Ever wonder why the Enemy doesn't want you to read the Bible? Has it ever occurred to you why your mind and body seem to get distracted or tired when trying to read the Word? It's not a coincidence. Why would the devil want you to easily read God's Word? Why allow your enemy to study the playbook that shows someone how to beat them and win?

Even though Hell has a dossier on us, God already knows who we are. He knows all the things Hell has against us, and God doesn't care. He already paid the price for the mess we've done and the stuff we will do before we take our last breaths. Here is my challenge to you. Everything that Hell doesn't want you to know, study, or understand in God's Word is exactly what you need to chase after! Whatever gives you difficulty understanding is exactly what you need to pray for and ask God to help you decipher the meaning and intention.

God is wisdom. God is all knowledge, and He will reward you for your level of hunger and thirst. The most dangerous person in the world is the one who doesn't have knowledge and doesn't want it. So many Christians choose to stay ignorant of the deeper things of God because they have been hindered by Hell's influence. Here is the sad part, some are hindered right in the Church with cult-like intensity. There are some ministries out there that are afraid of people who study beyond the pastor's understanding. Some traditions say that we just need to be good church people and not "poke the bear" and leave the Devil alone. A soldier afraid to fight is an unwilling, invisible ally to the enemy.

In the human world, knowledge is power. If people aren't aware of the power that Jesus Christ has given them, they won't know how to fight in this war. It reminds me of a meme that shows an elephant tied to a plastic chair and this great enormous beast sits there waiting. Tied to an invisible weight and fooled to think that there isn't a way out. Friends, let me reassure you that there is a way out. Jesus is the only answer and when He was about to leave Earth, He promised that the Holy Spirit would come and TEACH US (John 14:26). Why? Because He knew we would need it. That's why we need to pursue Godly knowledge and wisdom. It's how we will survive.

So, as you enter your prayer corner today, ask God to open your eyes. Pray that God takes the limits off of your life and then pledge to run after understanding. Pray that God uncovers the plot that Hell has to keep you blind to the truth. Pray to ask God to uncover the eyes of others around you. Pray that God gives you wisdom to see through the fog of war. Also, ask God to reveal to you the generational curses that may have you bound. God is a patient and loving teacher, so let Him lovingly lead you into all truths!

Day 23: Being Teachable

*A wise man is strong; yea, a man of knowledge increaseth
strength. For by wise counsel thou shalt make thy war:
and in multitude of counsellors there is safety. —
Proverbs 24:5-6 KJV*

Welcome to Day 23! I won't lie to you. Today's devotional is one of the hardest not only to write, but to live. I write this out of personal experience because I had a major point in my life where I wasn't teachable. At one time in my existence (as the old saying goes) it was a fact that once I had an idea in my head, not even dynamite could blast it out. I can admit that even today that I can get stubborn. We all can at some point and trust me when I tell you that God knows it too and is more patient than we would be.

There is an old country tale that has been told over the years about a time when people used mules to plow the fields. The story tells about an old mule that was fast, efficient, and obedient working. He was a joy to work with except for one specific time of the day. This mule didn't have a watch. He obviously couldn't read, and he didn't know how to tell time the way we do. However, this mule would stop whatever he was doing and lay down in the field around noon every day, and refused to work. It didn't matter where he was or what he was doing. Why? Because it was lunchtime. They said that when that mule was younger that the boys (and girls too) worked with the untrained mules because the older ones were sometimes too strong to be controlled. So when lunchtime hit everyone, and everything got to eat. This now old mule grew up knowing that and no matter how much you whipped him or pushed him he wasn't getting up until he got his food at noon like everyone else.

I know I laughed at that story because in our modern times it's hilarious. How did that old mule know it was noon? Who told him? He didn't care if there was another deadline to work past noon. He was the best at working and was great at doing what he did. He was strong and he was fast. He was effective and he was capable. Still, that mule wanted what he wanted and wouldn't compromise. He didn't get up until someone brought him food and when he got what he wanted; he got up and finished the day strong.

We are a lot like this mule. He probably grew up in a way and learned a trait and refused to compromise. A lot of us do the same thing spiritually. We grew up in a certain tradition or level of understanding and when it comes to something different; we don't want to budge or move until we are satisfied. Some of us refuse to get up at all because we think that we're in charge. I hate to tell you, but we are not in charge, but God is. Sometimes God requires us to work when He wants us to and not when we want to sit down. There are things God wants to show us, but we have to be teachable and receive them.

We can't be like that mule and sit down because we want things our way. We don't want to listen to this person because they aren't my pastor. We don't want to study this subject because it goes against what we grew up with. Some of us don't want to rock the boat of people around us with things God wants to teach us. We'd rather sit down and refuse to budge until we have our way. Friends, it won't ever work like that. See, God will whip us and encourage us to move beyond our boundaries, but He won't force us. He will be patient and urge us on, but it's up to us to get up from the field and keep working.

When I think about being taught, I am also reminded of my time in college. Professors would teach no matter if you paid attention or not. It wasn't like kindergarten where if you didn't pay attention, the teacher would stop, and you would be corrected. To graduate you need to make the grade. God is always ready to teach if we stop and listen. I remember some of my harshest professors that other people hated were the ones that were more passionate about learning. If I showed interest, they'd take extra time and show me more. The Word of God is an open book exam. We have the answers in front of us, but to get deeper wisdom we need to let the Teacher teach us. We need to submit and allow God to train us, shape us, and direct us. How much we want to learn is up to us. We should want to learn as much as we can and be at the top of God's Life Class.

So, as you enter your prayer corner today, pray that God lifts your stubbornness to dig deeper and learn more of Him. Ask God for forgiveness for not being willing to learn things you refused to see. Pray that God opens His heart to you and shows you what you need to know to fight the good fight. Ask God to show you how to do what He desires for you to do. Pray that God increases your desire to learn of Him and to learn from Him. Ask God to open your spirit to discern the truths He wishes you to see and the lies that you must abandon.

Day 24: Show Me Your Ways

Shew me Thy ways, O Lord; teach me thy paths. Lead me in Thy truth, and teach me: for Thou art the God of my salvation; on Thee do I wait all the day. — *Psalms 25:4-5 KJV*

Welcome to Day 24! Asking God to show us His ways is a humbling experience. As people, it is inherently difficult for us to admit that we need to change how we've been doing things. We get comfortable, settled, and pleased with how we have lived until we meet God for ourselves, and we see just how insignificant and misguided we have been. Once we have been brought into the Body of Christ, we are made aware of the true landscape of this life, and we are left with two choices: wander around hopelessly and let the Enemy sift us like wheat or ask God how we should move forward. What we've been doing hasn't been working and now it's time for a change.

I love old martial arts movies. Yeah, they might have corny sound effects and terrible props, but the stories they tell can be very revealing and most of them tell a tale that goes full circle and have a happy ending. Some of these stories will involve a typical young man who, through some misfortune, has to save the people that he loves. He tries to fight the enemies he encounters, but he is swiftly defeated and humiliated because he doesn't know how to fight their mastery of Kung Fu. In defeat and shame he runs away from his problems and many times travels into a distant country in self-imposed exile (or running for his life). It is then, through fate, he runs into a mysterious loner or an old man that seems ordinary who drops words of wisdom into his life, but is secretly a martial arts master and has the answers that the young traveler needs.

So what happens? Still licking his wounds, this young man begins to see that this old man is more than he appears. The young man sees how strong this old hermit is and begs that old man to train them in a new style of martial arts. Many times, the Master refuses to train them because they believe they want training for the wrong reasons. The student then goes above and beyond to prove that their cause is just and true. The new Master then puts the young man through a series of tests and trials. Sometimes the tasks seem mundane and quite stupid. At first, what the Master wants seems foreign and doesn't even make sense to the young student, but the more the student is dedicated to the Master's teaching the more the Master reveals to the student. Not just about fighting, but about life and how to live. Then, after a space of time, and seemingly hard work, the student is declared ready to go back and fight their enemies. The young man goes back, and his old foes laugh at him and remind him of how they beat him badly. The young man not only defeats them, but he rescues those he loves, and the movie ends happily.

When we receive the gift of salvation, we will get attacked by the Enemy. We may get beaten down for a while and many times want to give up. We will either sit in defeat or we will rise up and wonder how we can fight and win. We then seek the only one who can help us... God! We have to ask God to show us His ways, because God is above all. God knows how we have to be not just to fight the Enemy, but how to live in this life. We don't live to acquire personal power or gain. We ask God for His ways to succeed spiritually and to be all that God wants us to be. We need His training to accomplish the tasks He has set for us while we are assaulted by Hell. We are lost without Jesus, and we need His help to only thrive, but to survive. We need God's ways to live God's way.

So, as you enter your prayer corner today, ask God to show you His ways. Ask God to train you to win. Ask God to give you the strength to fight. Ask God to purge those habits and quirks that you have that are counterproductive to His Will. Ask God to lay out how you need to be trained and submit to His instructions. Pray that God gives you the discipline to do what He asks you to do, no matter how mundane it seems or how ridiculous to your flesh. Ask God to keep you in the land He has for you and that you will always try to be obedient to His Will. Ask the Savior to help you, comfort, strengthen, and keep you. He is willing to aid you and He will carry you through!

Day 25: The More You Know

*For in much wisdom is much grief: and he that increaseth
knowledge increaseth sorrow.* — *Ecclesiastes 1:18 KJV*

Welcome to Day 25! I'm sure that you read today's verse and wonder how in the world does this make any sense? Ecclesiastes was written by King Solomon, the wisest man who ever lived. This collection of wisdom was written near the end of his life and tries to capture all of what Solomon experienced throughout his days. Solomon had seen God work from the time he was born until the moments he recorded these verses. How can knowledge bring sorrow? How can much wisdom bring a ton of grief?

How many times have we heard a statement in a gangster movie that goes something like *"They know too much; someone is going to take them out"*? It works the same way in the spirit realm. The Enemy prefers an ignorant Christian because they are not a threat to him. He loves that shouting and dancing saint that has no spiritual power. He loves those in ministry who only tickle ears and soothe consciences. If we focus on the needs of the flesh, Satan won't bother us. A dead church won't come under attack if it stays dead. A Christian that doesn't grow is spared from trouble. If we are kept blinded from actual knowledge and wisdom from God, Hell doesn't waste resources on you.

The game changes the moment you hear from God and learn from Him. Hell pays attention to you. You crack that Bible open and read beyond the hype verses and clichés and demonic forces will try to distract you to put it down. The moment you take authority over the demonic power in your life Hell loads its guns and points them at you. You walk in the ways of Christ taught by the Holy Spirit and the attacks go from distractions to all-out assaults on your life and those you love. It never seems to end because the enemy is always watching. He is always scheming to take you down and finding new ways to do it.

Look at every ministry that woke up from slumber and started walking in the ways of the Lord. Divisions between people or ministries started up. Sickness attacked the people, sin tried to conquer folks and opposition against the truth rose. The crabs in the bucket start trying to pull other people down. People would start hearing the *"I remember when you used to..."* accusations start, and they never seem to stop. The secret cliques begin to plot other people's demise. The revelations of what was done in the dark get uncovered in the light. The realization comes apparent that the acquisition of spiritual knowledge or relationship leads the pain of Hell and sorrow right to their doorsteps. Some people give up and go back to the old ways that didn't get them attacked. The rest keep up the fight and earn new battle scars and stay in the war.

No one ever said that this journey with Jesus would be easy. The more we learn of Him, the more Hell ramps up its attacks on us. This is how it works. Hell has already lost the biggest battle that ended the war, which was when Satan lost at the Cross of Calvary. Every human conflict has had battles after the war was declared over. In the American Civil War, there were six battles after the Confederate surrender at Appomattox Courthouse.[8] Not one battle after Appomattox changed the result of the war already being won. Demons will still try to take you out because they want to take away just one more person from God's Army. That's petty and sadly that's real.

Let's remember that the Apostle Paul said near the end of his life in II Timothy 4:6-8, *"For I am now ready to be offered, and the time of my departure is at hand. I have fought a good fight, I have finished my course, I have kept the faith: Henceforth there is laid up for me a crown of righteousness, which the Lord, the righteous judge, shall give me at that day: and not to me only, but unto all them also that love His appearing."* Paul suffered pain for going from a murderer for the religious rulers to a preacher of Jesus Christ. Paul witnessed that there was a reward so we should stay in the pursuit of God's wisdom for us and keep walking in His knowledge.

So, as you enter your prayer corner today, ask God to increase your knowledge and wisdom in Him. Pray that God gives you the strength to withstand what will come your way to stop you. Ask God for protection of your mind, body, and spirit. Pray that God protects you and your loved ones because of the dirty tactics of Hell that will go for your throat. Remember... The more you know, the more you grow, and the more the Devil will hit you low!

---

[8] Klein, C. (2018, 31 August). *6 Civil War Battles After Appomattox.* https://www.history.com/news/6-civil-war-battles-after-appomattox

Part VI: God, I Am Yours

Day 26: I Belong To You

Know ye that the Lord He is God: it is He that hath made us, and not we ourselves; we are His people, and the sheep of His pasture. — Psalms 100:3 KJV

Welcome to Day 26! What a journey this has been! I pray that you have enjoyed this journey even though the realization of who we are in Christ is revealing and somewhat painful (in a good way) as we learned just where we stand with God. The verse for today sort of puts a cap on all that we've gone through on our discovery of a deeper relationship with Jesus. We belong to Jesus. God is our Father, and we are His children. We are the sheep of his pasture. There is power in knowing to Whom we belong.

Some time ago, I took one of those DNA tests to determine what my ancestry bloodlines were. The results were shocking to me. I had always been told about certain traits in my genes, but the test revealed absolutely none of those traits at all. It was shocking that I discovered that I was made up of things I never knew of or expected. It was a wake-up call to not only who I was, but those who came before me. It helped me connect some dots in my family history that now made sense because I knew more about myself. I knew more about the hidden secrets in my family. I knew where I truly belonged.

When we accept Jesus Christ as our Lord and Savior, we become grafted into the Family of God. Our spiritual DNA is fused with the Blood of the Lamb, and we become joint-heirs with Jesus Christ (Romans 8:17). When we realize that the spiritual DNA of Heaven flows through us who are saved, we will understand where we belong. God is our Father, and He loves His children (Ephesians 4:6). God made humanity from the beginning and even after Adam fell into sin, God launched a plan to restore us to Himself (I Corinthians 15:45). He didn't wipe us all out with a catastrophe like He did the first time. God didn't just snatch all of our breath away and kill us all. God pursues us and gives us a way back to Him. We didn't create ourselves. We can't even blink our eyes without God allowing it. We belong to Him.

As people of God, we need to make that declaration publicly that we belong to God. Our lives are not our own and we have no right to tell God what we're going to do against His Will even though He allows us to do so. From the bottom of our hearts and spirits, we need to confess to God that we are His. It's a powerful statement to put in the atmosphere. It notifies our flesh that God is our ruler and not ourselves. It declares to others around us that we are dedicated to living for God. It tells Hell that we know who we are and that we know who our Father is. We no longer serve our old master the Devil, and we belong to Jesus and Jesus alone. It's submission at the highest level. It's humbling and empowering. It unlocks so many possibilities in our relationship with God.

When two people enter a marriage they pledge their lives to each other. They declare in front of at least two witnesses that their promise is for real and out of true love. Jesus declared His love for humanity by dying publicly on the Cross. We as people don't have to openly accept Jesus Christ as our Lord and Savior, but we do declare the affirmation of our relationship in how we live each day. We don't have to shout it from the rooftops per se, but we do it by our prayers and worship. We do it by studying the Word and sharing that Word with others. We also do it by what kindness we show in private. It's a beautiful thing!

So as you enter your prayer corner today, confess to God that you belong to Him. Pour out your heart in gratitude that He spared your life to live for Him. Tell Jesus everything. Commit yourself in ways that you never have. Acknowledge that you are tied to God in a blood covenant that you never want to be broken. Ask God to give you the strength to be strong in your commitment. Know that even though you don't belong to yourself, God won't make you a robot automatically obedient to His every whim. Know that you still have a choice and that you freely choose Jesus over everything else!

Day 27: Gracefully Broken

*Woe unto him that striveth with his Maker! Let the
potsherd strive with the potsherds of the earth. Shall the
clay say to him that fashioneth it, what makest thou? Or
thy work, He hath no hands — Isaiah 45:9 KJV*

Welcome to Day 27! We are creatures of free will and God made us this way. This puts us in a unique position of all the life forms on the Earth. While they act on instincts, we act on instincts and rational thinking. We can choose every step we take, and we can fight our consciences or warnings that we see and understand. We have the ability, but that doesn't mean that we should. This is especially true when it comes to resisting the work of God in our lives.

What comes to my mind is (among all things) horse racing. I don't know a lot about horses, but I've picked up some knowledge along the way. From what I learned from some people is that horses are bred to be champions and they use the genetic materials from great racehorses to create offspring that have the potential to be great racers as well. What gives them that potential? Their physical attributes of muscle strength, eyesight, stamina, and intelligence. Many horses are bred this way, but few become champions. Why is that you may ask? The answer is simple... They couldn't be trained.

For a stallion to reach its full potential, it has to be "broken" of its will. Being broken is a grueling process meant to strip away independent thought and will. It requires the horse to go from rebellion to obedience to whomever commands the beast and coincidentally creates a bond of trust. They have to learn to trust the jockey who rides them and obey every instruction in order to become a winner. There are stables full of horses that are bred from great champions that can't be used to race because they refused to be broken. The horses that end up as winners recognize who is in charge and those horses develop loving relationships with their trainers. Even they know afterward that all of that pain they endured during being broken was worth it. I've yet to hear of a wild horse winning a major horse race. If you know of one, please let me know!

We as people are not horses, but God has to "break" us before we reach our full potential in Him. We may have gifts, talents, and abilities that God can use mightily, but if we are resistant to His Will and His Ways we are not any good to serve God effectively. We have to choose to surrender to the Holy Spirit and let Him gracefully break us and shape us into real champions for Jesus. Yes, the breaking, the shaking, and the beating do hurt, but it's all worth it. We have to be submissive to God as He works out our kinks. We have to freely and painfully let go of what God says to let go. We have to look forward to a deeper and loving relationship with Christ because all that He does to shape us is done in love and not in punishment.

Being gracefully broken means we are open to being exposed to God as needing training, too. Sin has cast a long shadow over our lives and God is so patient with us it boggles the mind. While the process may hurt, God will give us strength to endure it. He never gives us more than we can bear (I Corinthians 10:13) and His plan never fails if we push past our flesh and let God have His way in our lives. We can't cheat our way out if we really want to reap the benefits of God's loving, but harsh education. The strange thing about the horse example is that after being broken, that horse loves their trainer. After God breaks us, it strengthens our bond with Him. Isn't that wild?

So as you enter your prayer corner today, offer your surrender to God for whatever He desires for your life. Ask our God to gracefully break you and make over in His image. Ask God to give you the strength to be made over and made anew. Pray for God's direction as to where you have to go and what you must do. To say that *"I surrender"* means that you accept the call He has made for your life. To submit is to allow Him to mold you in His Hands. Stop running from God's process. Stop fearing what may happen. Pray that God gives you the patience to allow Him to work. Trust me, when you allow God to be God in your life you won't regret it. God will place you in the winner's circle every time.

Day 28: Save Me Lord

*I am Thine, save me; for I have sought Thy precepts. —
Psalms 119:94 KJV*

Welcome to Day 28! You may see the verse for the day and wonder what in the world does it mean that because if I am in a relationship with Christ, why do I need saving? The verse itself says *"I am yours, save me"* and it seems redundant until we get to the last part of the verse: *"For I have sought Your precepts"* and it becomes clear. When I read this verse, it reminded me that belonging to God comes at a price and we need to be rescued by God Himself because of it.

All the forces of darkness hate God because Lucifer was tossed out of Heaven. We all know this. Satan has done everything he can within his toolbox to block, stop, sabotage, and thwart the Will of God for humanity. The Enemy has potent weapons at his disposal, and he knows how to use them against us. We've talked about that before many times during this thirty-day journey. It's almost like we are used as collateral damage to hurt God when Satan takes the war he had with God out on us. When we seek the things of God, we break free from the lure and control of sin and trade those things for God's holiness.

The more we press into God, the more we have to be rescued when we fall short in our pursuit of God. We are still humans, and we will fail (Psalms 73:26). We all make mistakes no matter how long we've been a follower of Jesus. No one is immune to our failings of being in the flesh. Both God and Satan know how flawed we are. God knows it because He knows everything. Satan knows because he has stalked you from the moment you were conceived and took notes on everything we have ever done. He knows how the flesh can be stimulated and how our emotions can betray us. Thank God that He has a plan.

Part of belonging to God is knowing how much we can't live without Him. As we draw closer to God, we realize that knowing Him and needing Him are directly related. When we were in sin, we needed God to liberate us from death, but as we grow in His Grace, we also need Him to save us from ourselves and our messes. Because God never fails we can count on Him to hold us up even when we don't realize that we need His protection and His Love. There's no sense of sugar-coating the fact that the assault from Hell will get worse. It will never let up because as you chase God and grow in Him, you won't fall for yesterday's test. Job is the best example because Satan was allowed greater and greater levels of attack until God let Satan test Job within inches of his life.

The sinking of the *Titanic* was a horrible tragedy. Hundreds of people died because they believed that the ship that man had built was unsinkable. At that present time, the safety features that were built into it were game changing and never on any ships before. It was designed that if four of its watertight compartments would flood, the ship wouldn't sink. Sadly, six compartments had flooded, and they didn't have coverings over the tops of them and the ship filled with water and sank in just over two and a half hours and many people needlessly died.[9] Here's why… First, there weren't enough lifeboats and secondly (even for those who could swim) the suction of the ship going down was so strong that it pulled swimmers down with it. The waters were icy cold, and it was a disaster in the making. If it were a smaller ship, more could have survived. If its course wasn't through dangers, it would have completed the journey.

Spiritually, if we grow in grace to where we get too confident in our holiness we can still fall into our flaws or sins. The bigger our delusions are that we are unsinkable, we will be sucked under the waters when tragedy strikes. We need God to always keep us in line and to sometimes save us from ourselves as we chase after him. The Devil may lurk around us and try to destroy us, but we have to keep remembering that we belong to God. We need Him more and more as the days pass us by.

There is an alarming clarity that comes when we realize we need God on the level that we do. This is true not just when we were lost and in sin, but in every waking moment of our lives. We are literally like a wild ass on the loose (Job 39:5-8) and we need taming and saving from ourselves. I know we think we have it all under control, but sadly we do not. God knows this and loves us, anyway. It doesn't matter how long you have been serving God you will need to be saved from yourself and God knows it. The question is do you know it?

So as you enter your prayer corner today, pray that God shows you how much you need Him. Be overwhelmed at His massiveness and power. Tell God that you can't live without Him and that you will never try to ever again. Ask God to save you from yourself and all that you thought you knew. Ask God to help you understand more of the road ahead and what He wants for you to do and how He wants you to do it. Pray for more humility as you dig deeper into your relationship with Jesus. Ask God to show you every pitfall of the Enemy so that your foot won't slip and fall. Lastly, but not least, ask God to show you where you need more of His armor and more of His Wisdom.

---

[9] The Maritime Executive. (2017, May 3). *Watertight Doors Awareness Campaign Gets Underway*. https://www.maritime-executive.com/article/watertight-doors-awareness-campaign-gets-underway

Day 29: Facedown

*And all the angels stood round about the throne, and
about the elders and the four beasts, and fell before the
throne on their faces, and worshipped God, Saying, Amen:
Blessing, and glory, and wisdom, and thanksgiving, and
honor, and power, and might be unto our God forever and
ever. Amen. — Revelation 7:11-12 KJV*

Welcome to Day 29! As we know from our humanity, intimacy with God is a critical component of every relationship. Our connection to God works in the same way. Our God is amazing and is the embodiment of power. Jehovah God spoke creation into existence with simple words, and every intention, detail, and nuance was executed just because He spoke it. The Lord of the Universe, holder of all existence and Savior of the World, wants a relationship with each one of us puny, weakling humans. This is huge. This can't be dismissed by anyone.

Today's verse comes from Revelation, in which John the Revelator gets a glimpse into Heaven and witnesses something that I'm sure truly can't be captured with simple words. All the angels in Heaven along with the twenty-four elders proclaimed their adoration of God and fell on their faces in the worship of the King of Glory. This is a powerful display of these heavenly beings being overwhelmed by the Presence of God. It didn't matter who they were; they worshipped God. The Elders took their crowns off and fell before the Throne. I can only imagine what John must have felt at that moment. I know that he had to be overcome with the adoration of our God!

What I love about this scripture is that they weren't celebrating what God has done. They were just in awe of His power and His glory alone. They were moved in their hearts that there is no other God like our God. They worship Him for who He is. Their very existence depended on His Will. They were created by Him and without Him; they were nothing. Those elders were probably there when God spoke Creation into existence. I can imagine that all of this happened, and they remembered when Lucifer rebelled and took one-third of the angels with him. They had witnessed Jesus come through forty-two human generations to be born, live, and die for the sins of the world. They had seen it all and proclaimed their affection by bowing their faces to the Throne.

Every cell in your body belongs to God. The eyes you are using to read this devotional were created by Him. Every breath, every step, every thought, and every second of time belong to God. We did nothing to deserve existence. We were created from dirt and given a mind that could reason with the God of the Universe. God's existence alone deserves our worship. God, being who He is should pierce our souls and melt our hearts and nothing, but adoration should pour out of us. He made the Earth for us. He created the sun and the moon for us. He devised and implemented gravity to keep us on the ground. From the oxygen in the air or the waters of the sea, He made them for us!

We own nothing. Naked we came into this world and naked we shall leave it (Job 1:21-22). Everything we have, God allowed us to have it. We owe God everything. Our most clever thoughts and inventions are mere foolishness to God. We are tiny, weak, and defenseless and we, as humanity, messed up our relationship with God with sin. When He chose us to be His sons and daughters, our hearts should explode with thanks and love because He didn't have to do anything for us. He should have let us all die and go to Hell, but He loved us despite ourselves. What if God spoke again to erase us from existence? What if He had rebooted us as He did all of Creation between Genesis 1:1 and 1:2? He didn't and we all should be grateful.

Falling down on our faces before a Holy God transforms us in ways we can't imagine. We submit to God, and we fall face down because we aren't worthy of looking God in the eye as an equal. We may think that we are, but we are not in any shape or form. The power and majesty of God is indescribable. The immenseness of God is incalculable. God speaks and matter rearranges itself without blueprints. God breathes over corpses and the dead come to life. God moves in the Heavens and the Earth shakes in reverence. Who are we to think that we can stand before Him? What gives us the right to think that we can equal Him? We are literally nothing compared to God, and yet God knows our names. God is concerned about us and loves us. This same God who is bigger than us all Who came down to redeem the worthless. He came to save the lost. He calls us His friend. Knowing these things should cause us to fall on our faces and worship Him for such power and love.

So as you enter your prayer corner today, proclaim with a loud voice that you belong to God. Pray that God strips away any hindrance that keeps you from Him. Cast down your "crowns" which may be your position, your title or your self-imposed feelings of superiority. Pray for God's Everlasting Arms to wrap around you. Fall to your face and worship God. Cry out to Him because He is awesome, and He deserves all of our worship. Tell the Devil that you no longer belong to him or to sin. Let the Devil know you might mess up sometimes, but that you will never abandon God for Hell. Let it all out to God. Throw down your own crowns and worship God. He is ours and we are His forever and ever. He is our God and not like any other! Forever will we worship Him!

Part VII: God, I Thank You

Day 30: Hallelujah!

By Him therefore let us offer the sacrifice of praise to God continually, that is, the fruit of our lips giving thanks to His Name. — Hebrews 13:15 KJV

Welcome to Day 30! Congratulations! You made it through all thirty days of this connection or reconnection with our God. This isn't easy to go through and by God's Grace, you are here! The life of someone in ministry is never easy to live through, but our God always gives us what we need to not only survive but also to thrive. God has never left us alone and He knew that this wouldn't be easy for us. He sent His Son Jesus Christ to die for us; He sent His Holy Spirit to comfort us and His Word to teach us. For that, we can only be thankful for our God who has given us everything! Hallelujah!

Our God is so big, so wise and so powerful and He wants to get to know us tiny humans, spirits trapped in meat sacks, as a father knows and loves His children. I know I could go on and on about how good God is, and I know you could do the same. God is amazing and He deserves all the praise! Most people hear that and immediately think of raising their hands in church or making a joyful noise. That's not the only way to say thank you to God.

The sacrifice of praise is from the fruit of our lips. It comes from our spirits to our mouths, and it should be continuously flowing. I'm not saying that saying *"Thank You Jesus"* isn't enough. Our gratitude and praise to our God should come from all we do. What we say, how we act, how we witness, and how we worship should all show gratitude to God. I used to wonder why it said a sacrifice of praise until I lived a little and experienced some things. When Job lost his family, he praised God. When he lost his wealth, he praised God. Even when his friends challenged him, he praised God. Stephen glorified God with His dying breath. It's easy to thank God in church or during the good days, but what about the bad days? What about through the storms and rain? What about the failure and the pain? What about when you lose it all? What about when tragedy or heartbreak strikes?

A sacrifice of praise goes against human desire and emotion. To utter praises, no matter if it's good or bad is tough, but necessary. It goes beyond human logic to want to thank God when everything doesn't seem to be well. Through these thirty days, we've gone through so many things together. I'm sure that many of you have experienced attacks like you couldn't have imagined. I know that there have been good and bad days, but when we can still stand and say to God that He's still good and you thank Him something shifts in the atmosphere. Something also shifts inside of you. Chains fall away, doors begin to open, and situations change. The praise that used to hesitate on your lips is released quicker. That worship that you were afraid to let out busts through the doors of your heart. The deeper we go into a relationship with God we see why we do all of this. We see how much God loves us and we can't help but tell Him thank you!

The old adage about having an "attitude of gratitude" is keenly important when it comes to having a relationship with God. When we are thankful and grateful, something changes on the inside of us. What we focus on changes; what we desire changes. When we learn to see the good and the beauty in every situation and know that God hasn't left us or abandoned us, it transforms our heart. It opens our spirits in ways we never have before. We take our focus off of our stuff and our situation and turn it towards God and God alone. We see Him as the source of everything. It should break your heart wide open as it pours out the oil in our alabaster box.

This is what it's all about and why we do what we do for God. Even though humanity messed up big time, God gave us all a way back to Him. It causes one to be awestruck by how big God loves us and how powerful His passion for us is! It makes one speechless. Why would God do all of this for us? Why would He, the unlimited One, want a relationship with us? Why would He bless us when we deserved nothing from Him? That answer is all the way in the beginning. We were made in His image and likeness. He formed us personally and His Love never gave up on us. He redeemed the unredeemable. He saved the worthless by paying a great price so that we would have a right to eternal life! That should make your heart explode with joy! Our God wants us with Him forever and that's awesome!

So, as you enter your prayer corner today, tell God how much you love Him and that you will forever love Him. Tell Him thank You. Thank Him for the good and the bad. Thank Him for the happy and the sad. Thank Him for the broken road that you traveled. Thank Him for the days that you felt like He wasn't there, but that you know He was there all the time. Thank Him for every single tear you cried. Thank Him that you made it this far when you know you should have fallen by the wayside or died a long time ago. Thank God for every comeback after every setback. Thank God for His staying power and for the victories that you have won because He was an on-time God! Give Him praise and give Him glory for all that He was and is and is to come! Thank God for the chance to get to know Him better. Thank Him that He allowed us the space in time to commune with Him. This is just the beginning. Even though these have been thirty days of devotionals, there is still much more to explore in your walk with God. There are greater levels to reach in Christ. Thank God that He loves you so much to give you that chance!

THIS IS JUST THE BEGINNING

My sincerest prayer is that during the past thirty days that you have been forever changed by the power of the Holy Spirit. I hope God has spoken to you, revealed things to you in visions or dreams and that you have gotten hopelessly lost in His endless Presence. I believe God has refreshed you and prepared you for the journey that He has ordained for you to take forward. The passage that we take as we grow in our relationship with God never ends. The devotionals in Chapter Five are just thirty days out of your lifetime. God has blessed us all with (prayerfully) over thirty days to live and our pursuit should never be limited to a small space of time. We know the disaster our marriages and relationships would be like if we only worked on them for a month and then never wanted to go any further. A couple like that would die on the vine and possibly get distracted by someone else who pays more attention to them, and things will crumble.

God has promised that He would never leave us or forsake us (Deuteronomy 31:6) so the only one who would part from God would be us. Our God has promised in His Word that He would never stop pursuing us, but we are the ones with the potential wandering eyes and spirits. As humans, we are governed by our senses. As I've said before, we are in a relationship with a God we can't see or touch in the natural realm with a spiritual connection we have to forge. Our discipline in our walk with God must not get too comfortable, but it should now keep ramping up because Hell is still there, and Hell is still angry with you.

The fight won't end until you have breathed your last breath. We are a danger to the Enemy even on our deathbeds. Why? Because even while we are sick and immobile, we can still pray, and we can still be a witness to the power of God! The Apostle Paul was nearly blind towards the end of his life

111

and had to dictate his letters to his ministry partners. He even had to sign them with his own hand because I truly believe that others tried to send counterfeit writings to the churches he planted (2 Thessalonians 3:17).

In the last days of my dad's life he was basically bedridden and not the wellspring of vitality he was when he was well, but no matter who tended to him or visited him he always bore a powerful witness for Jesus. He inspired those around him even though this man who was mighty in his day was relentless in working for God. When he was younger, he could recite verses and teach the Word with authority. Even as he started to not remember every detail, Dad would write out whole note cards and keep them in his wallet. He never stopped loving Jesus or ever left the battlefield. Time may have taken his body and eventually his mind, but his spirit never stopped working. We shouldn't either.

This book is not the end, nor will it ever be the end. Where this may be a starter pistol for some folks, God has so much more for all of us. I'm sure of it and I pray you won't ever quit in your pursuit. We are like the soil of the earth. We can only bring forth fruit if we are disturbed from where we are season to season. When we ask the freshly tilled ground what happened, it would say a tragedy has occurred. To the farmer, it's an opportunity to plant and cultivate and the farmer never feels the need to apologize. The earth is disturbed and fussed over, treated for pests and weeds for a period. It's uncomfortable. I could imagine the farmer digging in it, walking on it, watering it, even covering it with fertilizer as they watch the plants growing and then finally harvests the crop.

Here is the beautiful thing about this example. Even after the harvest from the ground is collected, the farmer never stops working. The farmer plans for the next season of growth when the weather is workable for the crop they want to grow. So until then the earth rests while getting rained on, things die on and decompose and a few brazen plants may even show their roots in and start to grow until the farmer breaks that ground again for another season. It never stops as long as the farmer wants things to grow in the soil. The farmer won't always plant the same things there either. They rotate their crops to keep the soil healthy. It's a process that the dirt does not know how to do on its own.

God is our farmer. He knows what He wants to grow out of us. He has to stir us up season after season in our lives. One season, He may grow faith and in another He will grow wisdom. God knows what He wants from us, and He will till us, treat us and harvest from us what He knows is best for us. Pests will come for our harvest, but we have to let God tend to us. Purge us from the bugs and pull the weeds that try to grow in our spiritual soils.

Fertile ground is an invitation for pests and weeds. The Enemy is the prince of the powers of the air, and I imagine demonic forces are like seeds blown by the wind. A blown seed can't flourish in ground that isn't ripe for growth. Sure, a dandelion seed can sprout on damp concrete, but the sun will burn it up before it grows its first leaf. Also, if we don't tend our spiritual gardens something will eventually take root and next thing you know we are green and full of life from afar, but full of weeds up close. For God to use us again, He has to break our ground again. The longer we stay unattended, the more it will hurt for God to fix us up again.

Think about this for a minute. If God prepares you as a preacher of the Gospel and tills your spirit and plants that gift to grow, the weeds of pride, greed, deception, affairs, immorality, and the need for power could grow right alongside what God planted. For example, if God has planned for you to be a musician some of those same weeds could grow, including that record producer or secular opportunity that would poison your personal ministry.

Despite all of that, God knows, and He cares about us. He will give us second, third, fourth and infinite chances as long as we are willing to be groomed and prepared by Him. I would encourage you to stay within His plan because it's easier to stay obedient and open to correction than not be. The more our hearts are tuned into God the more likely we are to stay within His will and His way. God will always be patient with us, and we need to be patient with Him. God sees the bigger picture and He will always guide us right, even if it looks wrong at that moment. He sees around the bend where we can't, and we have to rebuke our fleshly mind and let go and let God.

Never stop learning and never stop doing all you can for God. Always be willing to run and chase after Him like your life depended on it because trust me when I tell you that it does. There are souls waiting on all of us to be an example of God's miraculous transformation power. It doesn't matter if you're struggling or not because we are all in God's process. No one has ever reached perfection in Christ. I remember in my math classes there is this concept called an asymptote. It's shown as a line on a graph for a mathematical equation. That line says that even as the numbers go to infinity, the graph of this curve will get closer, but will never touch it.

We will strive to be like God and adopt His ways, but we won't ever get there in these earthly bodies. We are still human and still full of flaws, and we can't quite reach the mark. God knows and He still loves us. If we give it our best, stay humble and stay repentant, God will work with us. This devotional series may have been your first journey into God, but I pray it's not your last. Keep pushing. Keep striving. God will always be there!

When God places you in the Refiner's Fire, don't despair, but know that regardless of what it seems like God will see you through it. The refining is meant to purify and cleanse you. The most precious gold is the metal that goes through the fire over and over. The strongest steel is heated red hot, and the slag scraped off again and again. God is a master artisan, and he knows how to get the best out of you. That means that instead of cowering in fear, be like Daniel and his friends. Walk around and don't be afraid. The

Son of God is with You.

Let's not forget your household, extended family, ministry group, and church family. No one is exempted from growing in Christ. Whomever you are connected to could be collateral damage in the attacks from the Enemy. We may not be able to control other people, but we can set an example to others that will show that growth in Jesus is not only worth it, but required. Hell won't stop ramping up against us. The Enemy and his demons are always watching us for opportunities. What do you think roaming about like a roaring lion looking to eat you up means? He's always in the hunt to knock you down and devour your spirit and he won't stop at just you. He will attack your family, your resources and even your health to slow you down or to discourage you.

So keep yourself covered under prayer. Keep your loved ones and ministry partners under prayer. Study the Word of God like you've never read it before. Never be comfortable with where you are in Christ. Anything that refuses to grow will die. It will get stagnant and will get infected. The Enemy wants you to stop and go no further. Hell wants you to never reach higher because if it can tame and shame you to stay put, the Enemy wins and Hell will run you over again and again. We can't allow that to happen. It's not just about us, but those who are still lost in their sins. We have a job to do and in God's Army and there are no reservists. We are all active-duty soldiers. The war may be over, but the battles will and must continue.

When it's all said and done, our journey with God is greater than we are alone. Someone out there is watching you. They see you and they know what you've been through, or they think they know. When we try to smile through our pain and live victoriously with the praises of God on our lips, a shift happens. We've all heard that expression that we may be the only Bible that some people ever read, and that's accurate. That's the truth. If we study and follow God's Word, it will ooze out of our spirits and it will shine a light all around you. How we live and how we are bears witness to what's inside. We can see a lamp in the dark because of the fire within. We know a stove gives heat because we can feel it when we get close to it. Our Sun is millions of miles away from us, but we can see its light and feel its warmth because we are in its orbit. People around us in their orbits will feel whatever light and heat we put out. Let it be our relationship with Jesus on display.

This means that we can't live any sort of way. We have an accountability that comes with serving in positions of ministry. We cannot be a worship leader helping to clean the atmosphere with the fragrance of worship on one hand and then practice sin on the other. We have to stay before God with clean hands and a humble spirit. We mustn't let our witness be tarnished by hidden sinful activities because we can contaminate our ministry without our sinful residue that we won't give over to God in repentance. This minimizes our effectiveness and also slanders the Name of God. I can't tell you how many people have been chased away from churches because of hypocritical ministry leaders. Not just pastors, but worship leaders, musicians and even ushers. We have to be better than that.

In my honest opinion, I truly feel that we have to be the light of the world in ways that were established in the beginning and be that light for Jesus relentlessly. The Early Church didn't have social media, television or printed materials like we do now. They reached people where they were and where they went and told people their personal accounts of how they met Jesus. I think in a lot of ways we've lost that fire and desire. Our church buildings, denominations and organizations are important, but The Church also needs to get out there where the lost souls are and show the way. The Light of God can't just shine on Sunday from a certain address. Sure, we may not shine as brightly by ourselves, but one lit candle can be seen from a great distance in the dark as a place of safety.

So many churches have become popularity centers, fundraising committees and country clubs instead of being the hospital for the spiritually sick, the bountiful blessing for the poor, the shelter for the homeless, the rescue for the abandoned, and the training center for ministers of the Gospel. No, it's not the "photo op" style of ministry that's important to the Spirit, but the kind that runs into someone at the gas pump when you see someone's card declined and you buy them some gas. It's the kind of ministry that gives a meal to a hungry family and doesn't post it on social media for likes. It's the kind of ministry that sees someone who looks down or out to tell them with compassion that Jesus loves them.

God created us so that His Light can shine through us. We are like wires. Think about this for a moment. We have seen the lights of Broadway, Las Vegas and even Tokyo either in-person or through images. All the dazzling colors, patterns, and displays are a feast to the eyes and pierce the darkness with an inescapable light. Whether it be standard incandescent light bulbs or LEDs every single one of them cannot make that light by themselves. They all need power and to get that power they need some form of wire. Little LEDs are small and have little thin wires while spot and flood lights need thicker wires, but regardless of what they are they shine brightly because of the wire that connects them to the power source.

We can't be that light until the Fire of the Holy Spirit burns deep within us. We can't have that Fire until we go through the fire. With the Fire comes purging and purification. That strengthens our witness. We can't be a witness to the Light until we know what the icy darkness feels like. We can't tell someone who is in distress that help is on the way if we've never been in dire trouble before. Our journey with Jesus makes us living and breathing proof that the God that can be seen by human eyes is alive in the human world. That is why we need to let go and let God. It's not for us at all in the grand scheme of things. It's so that God gets the glory for His amazing power. It's because we as humans believe nothing we can't see for ourselves. It's just how the flesh works, and we need to understand it.

This isn't a guilt trip, but a call to repentance and embrace all of what God offers us. When we see the big picture, we should never want to do anything less than serve God and live a life that He would be proud of. This consecration journey is geared to realign your mind, body, and spirit into a closer proximity to God's desires and wishes for our lives. We that want to be used need to realize that we don't set the conditions, but God does. Not a church house or pastor, but God speaks for Himself in His Word. When we invite Him into our lives, hearts and spirits, we allow the Holy Spirit to not be our co-pilot, but our pilot, navigator, and the vessel we travel in to get where He has for us to go.

For some of us, this is something that we haven't ever been taught before. It's something that sadly many churches don't explain. I'm not throwing stones when I say this because there is a real and active movement to get back to those ways that Scripture illustrates. Be a part of that Movement. Be a Heaven-sent activist for God's Truth and not just a doctrine or tradition. Be a witness and an active participant. This is our destiny to reflect the Light of God and Truth as He works through our lives. Don't fear and be courageous because the battle is not yours, but belongs to God!

The core of this book is about consecration and, believe it or not that never ends. When God passes one mantle to us, it doesn't mean that we are done, and our job is finished. No, many people in ministry were consecrated and set apart for one field in ministry only to have to take up another by the Will and Grace of God. Never, ever be satisfied with just being on the first floor of this Kingdom Building. For every flight upwards we take, God will have more in store for us to do, but He won't force you up those stairs. God always bids us to come to Him, but it is our choice to take that step with Him and take His Hand. We don't need to know what the future holds as long as Christ holds the future. Our level of trust and devotion to God should continue to grow off the charts, because God is eternal, and He is endless.

Let God set the limits of your ministry and your consecration. Let God show you where to walk and where to pause. Never let fear rush in to slow you down or stop you from your potential in Christ. As long as God says to go forward? Go forward. Trust His Voice and trust His Will for your life. We need to stop trying to take "the wheel" and truly let Jesus have it all. Give God all the control and let Him show you the way. Don't let the Enemy intimidate you into backing down. That fire that is in your heart and soul requires refreshing constantly. The Holy Ghost is ready and willing to revitalize your spirit. Let Him do what He does best.

When we let God do His perfect work in us, we are forever transformed and renovated by His Power. Worship Leaders (and other workers in the Ministry) need this consecration and development to be effective for God's use. We can't breathe out what we haven't breathed in. We cannot minister, teach, sing, preach or pray unless God puts something inside of us. If God didn't put it in our spirit, it is HUMAN MADE and while God can still use it for His Glory, it can't be as effective as if He placed those gifts, talents, ministry, and power into us.

Worship Leaders cannot lead worship without a worship life and a strong bond of communion with God. Preachers and Teachers can't preach and teach unless they receive God-sent preaching and teaching. Prayer Warriors cannot be effective intercessors and deliverance workers unless they bombard Heaven on their own and have a close relationship with the Holy Spirit. Once cannot be a ministry leader unless they were a faithful ministry follower and worker. I truly believe that God gives us gifts as the starting line of our journey and waits for us patiently to let Him develop and grow in us what He planted from the beginning.

Consecration is a part of that process that tells God that "I'm ready" to be set apart, worked on, poured into, and developed into what God has planned for you. Yes, we will lose our will to His. Yes, we will become willing vessels with little control over what we do for the Kingdom. Yes, we will suffer loss and persecution, but when you stop and think about it… Isn't it all worth it? It is and time and time again He proves it!

Don't you dare stop pressing into God for what He desires for your life and ministry. It doesn't matter what season of life you may currently be experiencing I ask that you trust God in the process that you are being put through. I know that we've talked about seasons many times in this book, but there is one final thing about seasons that I want to share with you. Your season is not about what's happening around you, but your POSITION. Look at the Earth for a moment. The seasons change not according to the weather, but where the planet is in its rotation around the Sun.

Your season isn't about the spiritual "weather" you are experiencing but the position that you are in hat God has allowed. Don't look at your circumstance and think that this is where you are in your walk with God. No, look at the position God has placed you in. Look at where you are serving. Look at the lessons that you have or haven't learned yet. Look at the people around you and the situations that they are in. Most importantly, if you don't know what position you are in ask God to reveal it to you.

Your consecration period may come during a season of lack or it might come in a season of harvest. No matter what it is or what's happening stay focused on your spiritual position. It can and will have an impact on your life and your personal ministry. Only trust God and only stay close to His Word. Now that you have dedicated yourself to Him like you haven't before don't let go and don't let up. Don't lose this newfound zeal and excitement because the letdowns and attacks are going to escalate and hit you where you have never been hit before. God has your back and won't let you fail!

God won't let you fall, and it is important to keep fighting sin in your life and keep resisting the temptations that will come. Don't let the little foxes spoil the bunch. I can't say it enough that you have a big target on your life right now. No matter how far you go in God it only takes one small misstep to fall down. Yes, you can get back up, but what will the cost be? Is it worth the risk? Is it worth it you to practice a sin and lose what God has given you? Look, I am not saying that you have to be perfect, but be holy AS Christ is holy. We can't be like Him, but we can do our best and seek God for the rest.

Finally, as you have come to the end of this little book, I want to leave you with this, my prayer for you as you continue on your spiritual journey:

May Yahweh, the God of Israel, bless you, your home, your family and everything you touch for the rest of your days.

May His Face shine upon you and give you and your loved ones peace.

May His Holy Spirit fall upon you even now, like the dew rests upon the blades of grass in the morning.

May His Fire be sprinkled from His Altar upon you to purify your spirit.

May His Hands hold you close and protect you from all dangers seen and unseen.

May God continue to lead you and guide you into all truths.

May God continue to chase after you as you relentlessly chase after Him with love and adoration.

May God richly anoint your mind, your body, your spirit, and your heart with His unlimited power.

"Now unto Him that is able to keep you from falling, and to present you faultless before the presence of His Glory with exceeding joy, to the only wise God our Savior, be glory and majesty, dominion and power, both now and ever." Amen! (Jude 24-25)

About the Author

Sean R. Foster is worship leader, musician, poet, songwriter and teacher who has dedicated his life to the advancement of the Kingdom of God. He currently serves as a Minister of Music and has been a Worship Team Leader. He also has ministered in many churches in the Mid-Atlantic Region. He has been involved in music ministry for nearly thirty years as a choir member, worshipper, choir director and instrumentalist, serving wherever God has called him to be. Mr. Foster has mentored and taught many worship leaders and musicians via the classroom setting and from the podium by the request of organizations seeking to grow their Music Ministries. He is a Virginia native who is happily married to his beautiful wife, who is the love of his life, and enjoys spending time with his family, studying The Word, reading books on various subjects, playing video games and watching Doctor Who.

www.ingramcontent.com/pod-product-compliance
Lightning Source LLC
Chambersburg PA
CBHW031535040426
42445CB00010B/544